The profound temptation of pastoral ministry is to slip into a role—the professional pastor, the passionate preacher, the wise counselor, the able administrator—and find our real selves divorced from our calling. If you find this happening to you, then this reminder from Brian Croft and Jim Savastio is a bracing and yet hopeful reminder that the pastor's soul is the very lifeblood of his ministry. And yet, self-care and soul-care is not simply taking two Bible verses each morning and going off to work. It involves use of the means of grace, paying attention to one's body, caring for one's family, and engaging in the shared leadership of the church with trusted fellow elders. If you want to survive and thrive in ministry, Croft and Savastio show you the way!

— DR. SEAN MICHAEL LUCAS, SENIOR PASTOR, INDEPENDENT PRESBYTERIAN CHURCH (PCA), MEMPHIS, TENNESSEE AND CHANCELLOR'S PROFESSOR OF CHURCH HISTORY, REFORMED THEOLOGICAL SEMINARY

Paul admonished Timothy—and pastors in the 21st century by extension—to keep a close watch on his life and doctrine. Pastors have never faced more dangerous challenges to their well-being and, thus, it's never been more difficult to keep a watch on one's heart and mind. Croft and Savastio have written a desperately-needed volume for desperate times. With ministers failing and leaving ministry, never to return, at an alarming rate, pastor, get this book and hear and heed its vital message. If you are not a pastor, read this book and learn how desperately your pastor(s) need your prayers and encouragement.

— JEFF ROBINSON, SR., LEAD PASTOR, CHRIST
FELLOWSHIP OF LOUISVILLE AND SENIOR EDITOR,
THE GOSPEL COALITION.

Pastors must take care of their own souls if they want to shepherd their congregations well over the course of ministry. Brian Croft and Jim Savastio have drawn from their own experience to produce a resource in *The Pastor's Soul* that is biblical, encouraging and practical. Every minister of the gospel will benefit from this thoughtful book.

— ROBBY GALLATY, SENIOR PASTOR, LONG HOLLOW
BAPTIST CHURCH, FOUNDER, REPLICATE MINISTRIES

It is all too easy to press on in our working for God but to slow down in our walking with God. Many books about gospel ministers and their ministry focus on the first, and risk becoming mechanical and distant. By contrast, this book speaks not generally but specifically to the life and soul of the pastor. It is full of pointed, personal, sometimes painful, truly profitable counsels, written by two brothers in the Lord who have proved the truths they now communicate to us. It digs beneath the surface to clarify personal and pastoral priorities. It calls us back from self-reliance and manic activity to dependence on God and stable service. However long you may have been on the way and in the ministry, it provides not just a frame of reference for the work, but a spiritual health-check for the worker. Humbly and wisely heeded, this warm and lively book should prompt spiritual longevity and prosperity in God's servants, and therefore help bring God's blessings to those they serve.

— JEREMY WALKER, PASTOR OF MAIDENBOWER
BAPTIST CHURCH; AUTHOR, *A PORTRAIT OF PAUL*

*The Pastor's Soul* serves the local church and the local church pastor very well. Pastors Croft and Savastio have helpfully addressed the pertinent issues in the lives and souls of the men God has called to shepherd His people. The careful attention to the spiritual realities of watching after yourself as well as the responsibility of caring for others left me wanting to give increased attentiveness to the care of my own soul. The balance of consideration for both spiritual well-being and physical health is refreshing as well as convicting.

— **ANTHONY MATHENIA**, PASTOR OF CHRIST CHURCH, RADFORD

Robert Murray M'Cheyne, a great Scottish preacher of the 19th century, died at the age of 29. Recognizing that his own lifestyle largely contributed to his failing health, he cried, "God gave me a message to deliver and a horse to ride. Alas, I have killed the horse and now I cannot deliver the message!" *The Pastor's Soul* is written to prevent such a cry today. Such a book should be read at least once a year by every pastor as an all-important health check. Too many good men short-circuit their ministries due to failure to care of themselves.

— **CONRAD MBEWE**, PASTOR OF KABWATA BAPTIST CHURCH AND CHANCELLOR OF THE AFRICAN CHRISTIAN UNIVERSITY IN LUSAKA, ZAMBIA

# THE PASTOR'S SOUL

# THE PASTOR'S SOUL

## THE CALL AND CARE OF AN UNDERSHEPHERD

### BRIAN CROFT
### JIM SAVASTIO

Copyright © 2018 by © Brian Croft and Jim Savastio

First published in Great Britain in 2018

British Library Cataloguing in Publication Data
A record for this book is available from the British Library

Print: 978-1-78397-238-8
Kindle: 978-1-78397-239-5

Evangelical Press (EP Books), an imprint of 10Publishing
Unit C, Tomlinson Road, Leyland, PR25 2DY, England

www.epbooks.org
epbooks@10ofthose.com

# CONTENTS

*To Bill Hughes and Austin Walker, two of the most faithful pastors, enduring godly examples, and most significant influences in our lives.*

# ACKNOWLEDGMENTS

**Jim would like to thank...**

**Cathy Vail Britt.** I promised long ago that if you were successful in helping me marry your sister that I would one day dedicate my first book to you. I need to be a man of my word. Thanks Cathy!

**Pastor George McDearmon** (whose ministry brought me to faith in Christ as a teenager and who discipled me in those pivotal early years) and **Pastor Albert N. Martin** who mentored me on what a faithful ministry looks like behind and outside the pulpit. The benefits of your investment are incalculable.

**Bob, John, James, Ryan, Rick, Charlie, and Derek** who have labored beside me in the eldership through the decades. Thank you for your ministry to me and the precious flock of RBC Louisville.

**Brian**, my writing partner, for asking me to join you on this project.

**Brian would like to thank...**

**David Murray** for writing such a meaningful foreword and for your years of friendship and investment in me.

**Rob Gibson, Bob Hudson,** and **Eric Johnson**, for without your friendship and diligent, skilled effort to care for my broken and weary soul throughout the last 5 years, I am convinced I would have lost it all.

**Micah Childs** and **Bob Stewart** for reminding me of the indispensable gift it is to have regular meaningful friendships with men who love and accept me as the broken sinner I am.

**Jim**, for your friendship and partnership in this book as well as the many ways I get the honor to serve with you in this ministry.


**Brian and Jim would like to thank...**

All those who read drafts of this book at different stages and made it better. Special thanks for the efforts of **Spencer Harmon** and **Randall Cofield** in this regard.

**Jeremy Walker** for your meaningful friendship to us, your encouragement of this book, and your initiative you took with us to publish with Evangelical Press. We trust this to be a fruitful partnership for many years to come.

**The Board of Practical Shepherding** for your support, friendships, and encouragement of this project.

**Auburndale Baptist Church** and the **Reformed Baptist Church of Louisville** for allowing us the distinct pleasure of shepherding your souls as we seek to care for our own.

**Our wives** and **children** who unconditionally love and support us despite the way our wrecked souls bring havoc on our families at times. Thank you for allowing the Lord to use you to be a healing balm to our weary souls and a place of rest from the rigors of ministry.

**The Chief Shepherd, Jesus Christ**, who saved us by his blood, keeps us, loves us, and cares for our souls in such a way that we can now go serve Him as his undershepherds.

# FOREWORD

## 'The minister's soul is the soul of his ministry'

'The minister's soul is the soul of his ministry.' I can't remember where I first heard this saying, but I've never been able to forget it. And, having read this book, I never want to forget it. In these pages, Jim Savastio and Brian Croft establish the foundation of all faithful and fruitful ministry—the pastor's soul. But, although their main target is the epidemic of ministerial hyper-activity and the accompanying burnout, backsliding, and brokenness, they carefully avoid over-reacting and running to the opposite extremes of monkish withdrawal or lazy self-indulgence. Instead, you have a book that skillfully walks a balanced biblical path in both content and style.

It balances self and others. Yes, the pastor is all about serving others, about sacrificing for the sake of others, about spending and being spent for others, and about pouring out themselves to fill others. But, as many pastors have discovered to their cost and pain, servants are finite, sacrifices eventually turn to ashes, non-stop spending leads to bankruptcy, and pouring out without ever filling up ends in drought. This book reminds us that caring for self is not selfish but necessary if we are to sustain a life of caring service to others. It's not a warrant for sloth or selfishness, but rather a call to self-care that will lead to better other-care.

It balances the soul and the body. While the spiritual life of the pastor is their primary concern, Brian and Jim do not fall into the trap of gnostic dualism—belittling the body and focusing exclusively on the soul. Yes, the soul is prioritized, and spiritual life is at the core, but the authors recognize not only that our souls impact our bodies, but our bodies also influence our souls. You'll therefore find not only wise shepherding of our souls, but also a concern for how we sleep, eat, exercise, and so on.

It balances relationship with God and relationship with others. This book encouraged me to go deeper, longer, and wider with God. I came away from it with a hunger and thirst for renewed friendship with my heavenly Father, my Savior, and my Sanctifier. But I was also motivated to pursue deeper, wider, and longer friendships with others. As the authors emphasize, this begins with a pastor's wife and children, but they also prove the necessity of more godly male friends in the pastor's life.

It balances biblical instruction and personal illustration. The foundation of this book is biblical exegesis as it tours numerous key verses to mine them for all that God has to say to pastors about their own soul care. But it also incorporates numerous personal examples of how Jim and Brian have experienced the truth of this teaching in their long pastoral ministries. Their transparency and vulnerability about their failures and successes bathe the book in authenticity. Pastors will clearly sense that the authors have been in the trenches of ordinary everyday pastoral ministry and bear many genuine scars and carry a few medals for valor. You'll find reality, but not a reality show.

It balances big-picture principles with detailed practical application. A few big truths will emerge throughout this book, important theological principles that stand out demanding attention and meditation. But how do we connect them with our lives? How do we bring them down from their lofty theological heights and into contact with Sunday through Saturday ministry? That's where this book excels. It takes deep doctrine into the details of daily pastoral life. Theory becomes intensely and intimately practical.

It balances challenge with do-ability. Some pastoral ministry books aim so high that their impossible standards paralyze and depress us. Others set such a low bar that the ministry is diminished and the dignity of the pastoral calling is tarnished. This book lifts the bar high but not out of sight. It promotes a high view of gospel labor and demands high standards, but not in a discouraging way that ends up limiting gospel ministry to supermen. At times, you will exclaim, 'Who is sufficient for these things?' But you will quickly respond, 'My sufficiency is of God' (2 Corinthians 2:16; 3:5).

It balances gospel repentance with gospel hope. No pastor will read this book without repenting. Tears of contrition will stain the pages (or ruin your Kindle!). But it doesn't end there. Brian and Jim apply healing gospel balm to the deepest wounds of conviction. And it doesn't end there either. They go on to entice and encourage us with the prospect of a much healthier and happier ministry ahead. Yes, it can be different. The past does not have to be repeated. There's a different and better way of being faithful in this calling. It doesn't have to be all about grit and grind until early retirement or even earlier death.

Yes, you will see blue lights and hear wailing sirens if your busyness and stress have made the presence of God in your life a distant memory. But you will also sense the prospect and possibility of a much better kind of ministry life—one that doesn't hollow out your heart, run down your body, or jeopardize your most important relationships. This is a hopeful and hope-filled book that can change the trajectory and tone of your entire ministry.

Thank you, Jim and Brian, for writing such a biblical and balanced book. My earnest prayer and fervent hope is that God will use it to rescue many pastors from the wrecker's yard and prevent multiple others from ending up there. May God bless your labors so that pastors everywhere will experience that a revived soul is the key to a revived ministry.

Dr David Murray, Professor of Practical Theology, PRTS,
Author, *Reset: Living a Grace-Paced Life in a Burnout Culture*
March 2018

# INTRODUCTION

There is immense pressure for pastors today to act super-human. After all, there are sermons to write, meetings to lead, widows to care for, the sick to visit, leaders to train, souls to counsel, members to disciple, Greek to study, ministries to run, and conflict to resolve. Then, there is a wife to love and serve, kids to care for, homework to do, toddlers to chase, teenage boundaries to set, music lessons to have, sport's practices and games to attend, yards to keep, bills to pay, pets to feed, and cars to fix. And with whatever time is left—friends to engage, family to visit, trips to take, cookouts to attend, and board meetings to tolerate. Simply making that list wears me out. And yet, this is how so many pastors function in their day to day life. The pastor runs crazy from sunrise to sunset, with little or no margin for the unexpected and most importantly—for himself.

In an incredible irony, many pastors spend their life pouring themselves out for the care of others with little or no regard for the need to care for themselves. Almost always there are consequences. Sometimes they are disastrous. Just within the last six months I have been involved with pastors whose marriages imploded. Pastors who committed suicide. Pastors who had nervous breakdowns and deep dark depression. Pastors who experienced stress induced strokes and heart attacks. In every case, there was one common thread—a neglect of personal soul care.

There appears to be two reasons pastors neglect their own soul. First, pastors get so caught up in the task and pressures to care for others. A good quality in many pastors is the zeal and deep conviction God's undershepherds feel to embrace the call of the Chief Shepherd—to shepherd the flock until he returns (1 Peter 5:2-4). Pastors are to fulfill this calling sacrificially, faithfully, humbly, and diligently. However, nowhere in Scripture does God call a shepherd to neglect his own soul to do so. In fact, Paul says the opposite when he exhorts the Ephesian elders to, "Keep watch over *yourselves* and all the flock" (Acts 20:28 NIV). Pastors too often allow themselves to be consumed and lost in this noble work on behalf of the Chief Shepherd that we forget to care for ourselves.

Second, pastors neglect their own souls out of fear of what they might find there. Most of us have learned the best way to avoid our own problems is to focus on someone else's problems. Then add to that dysfunction an extreme busyness that assures we don't stop long enough to realize the pain of our own lives and the starvation of our own souls for God and his presence. Pastors who feel the ever-present pressure to do everything right and have it all together are afraid to look deep in the darkest places in their souls. They are terrified of what they might find. Instead, they just perform. They put up the façade their churches expect. They smile and preach. And they keep pressing on in the work of the ministry while the soul slowly dies inside. We keep pressing on, that is, until the crash comes. The wake of those waves is often very painful and sometimes devastating.

This book aims to help pastors now, before the waves crash; to give hope to pastors who are already swimming in the remains of the crash trying to put the pieces back together. This book calls all pastors to step out of the shadows of busyness and artificiality, to courageously stop and take an honest look into who they are before God. This book challenges every pastor to consider that a strong, authentic, and powerful ministry comes first from an intentional commitment to care for one's self before caring for others. We advocate the engagement of four primary areas of care that need to be engaged for lasting results: biblical, pastoral, spiritual, and physical.

These areas of care comprise the four primary divisions of this book. Jim and I have divided the task to address these four areas with the hope you will benefit from both our voices, voices that come from different backgrounds and experiences. And yet our voices eventually meet in the middle where we are convinced is the only place to find care, healing, and hope for the pastor's soul. Read and take a moment to let go. Let go of the pressures to care for others. Let go of the fear to take a deep look. See what is there. Invite Jesus to that place. Receive his grace that is as abundantly available to you as it is for those for who you labor so faithfully.

*Brian Croft, January 2018*

# PART I

# BIBLICAL COMMANDS CONCERNING A PASTOR

JIM SAVASTIO

# 1

## TAKE HEED TO YOURSELF

It happened again this week. No doubt you heard the news about the pastor who left his church due to immorality or being burned out. Depending on your status, you may have received the news with a shrug of the shoulders or with grief or perhaps you have taken it as a providential shot across your bow. It could have been you. Maybe it should have been you. You may be taking up this book with a sense that you are barely hanging on. Perhaps for months there has been little genuine spiritual vitality in your personal life. You feel like you have been running on fumes as you preach a Christ whom you have not personally treasured for some time. Perhaps you have failed again in some area of moral or relational compromise. You've told yourself repeatedly that it has to stop, or it will mean the end of your ministry, and yet you've gone on feeling either defeated, condemned, or worse, hard hearted. It may be that you have decided to read this book with hope that it will help you to hang on for a few more months before another assignment comes your way.

The fact of the matter is, you have grown weary in well doing (Galatians 6:9). The thought of another elders' meeting, or congregational meeting is causing you distress and depriving you of needed rest and Christian joy. It is feeling like every other day is Sunday and you know full well that that next passage will not exegete or preach itself. You are convinced that the pressures of ministry are unrelenting. It's quite possible I have not described you. You may be in the midst of new and flourishing ministry. It may be that the Lord has been dealing very graciously with your soul and things have never been better. I'm thankful. I wish I could tell you that you will never enter a dark valley again. If you live and minister long enough in this old cursed world the pressures of ministry will hit you at some time.

In his first lecture to his students, Pastor Charles Spurgeon addressed the theme of the 'Minister's Self-Watch.' The so-called Prince of Preachers knew not only great public success, but spoke often and passionately of the private life that was the well spring of such public power.

> It will be in vain for me to stock my library, or organize societies, or project schemes, if I neglect the culture of myself; for books, and agencies, and systems, are only remotely the instruments of my holy calling; my own spirit, soul, and body, are my nearest machinery for sacred service; my spiritual faculties, and my inner life, are my battle ax and weapons of war. M'Cheyne, writing to a ministerial friend, who was traveling with a view to perfecting himself in the German tongue, used language identical with our own: I know you will apply hard to German, but do not forget the culture of the inner man—I mean of the heart. How diligently the cavalry officer keeps his saber clean and sharp; every stain he rubs off with the greatest care. Remember you are God's sword, his instrument—I trust, a chosen vessel unto him to bear his name. In great measure, according to the purity and perfection of the instrument, will be the success. It is not great talents God blesses so much as likeness

to Jesus. A holy minister is an awful weapon in the hand of God.[1]

## Understanding Yourself

What does it mean to take heed to yourself and in what way is this fundamental pastoral duty an aid to your perseverance and joy in ministry? Is it possible to endure the trials and tribulations that attend a faithful ministry? The Apostle Paul believed it was. He told the Ephesian elders that despite the persecution that he knew was coming his way that he looked forward to finishing both his race and his ministry that Jesus had given him with joy (Acts 20:24). Not without chains and not without tribulation, but with joy. How? Is it possible for men to maintain their purity and integrity and their joy all the days of their ministry? I am not talking about sinlessness nor am I speaking of a ceaseless 'mountain top experience.' But I am also not talking about growing callouses or developing a cynical edge that distances you from emotional harm. Can we maintain a vibrant communion with the living God, a love for the word and a love for the Lord's people over the long haul? I am being bold to declare that the answer is yes. The means are clearly laid out in God's word and available to every gospel minister. In writing to his young pastoral protégé, Timothy, the Apostle Paul writes:

*Take heed to yourself* and to the doctrine. Continue in them, for in doing this you will save both yourself and those who hear you (emphasis mine, 1 Timothy 4:16).

'Take heed to yourself' is not a suggestion. It is a command to be embraced all day and every day. The term 'take heed' is fleshed out in various translations as 'pay close attention to yourself' or 'watch yourself' or 'keep a close watch on yourself.' To put it another way, don't ignore yourself. What are we to make of this apostolic exhortation? Are not godly men in ministry to be marked by selflessness? It is important to know Paul is not contradicting himself with this command to pastors.

In what way, then, is it righteous to pay attention to yourself? While a man is not to obsess over himself, he is to be aware of who he is, how he is doing, and why. He ought to know the state of his own soul. He ought to have some means of gauging his walk with Christ, his integrity and his heart towards others. He ought to be able to answer in the theater of his own conscience or under the loving interaction with his wife or a fellow laborer, 'How are you really doing?' The issue here is not how good or effective your preaching is; it is not what your reputation with others is. The question has nothing to do with the size of your church but with you—as a man. The first issue is not whether my decline is noticeable to others and has affected my public ministry, but who am I and what am I before God when no one is watching?

## Who Am I?

I want to take a moment to address this question of "who am I?" I want to take up the issue of your identity. Here are three things to encourage you to think through and deal with before God.

## I am a Man

The first thing that you must understand about yourself is that you are only human. In Psalm 103 the writer is exhorting himself and others to a daily, robust, heart-felt praise to God in light of who he is, what he has done, and is doing for us. He is mindful that there is a disconnect in his life between his very good theology and his experience. If God is so good and merciful and forgiving and generous, how can I withhold praise from him? To aid him in stirring his heart to whole-souled adoration, the writer enumerates the blessings which God has poured out upon him and all the covenant people. Among these blessings is how God views us in our humanity.

As a father pities *his* children, So the LORD pities those who fear Him. For He knows our frame; He remembers that we are dust.

— PSALM 103:13-14

In all his dealings with his children God keeps in mind that we are dust. In the verses that follow there is something of an exposition of what this means. It means that we are temporal, frail, weak, and even dying. We are not supermen. We do not have a limitless capacity for labor and service. We grow weary and faint. We are limited in our ability to understand and communicate truth to others. We are limited in our ability to do good to others. We are, in the sight of God, like the little children of a master artist who cannot color between the lines. The Father knows this about us. It is not for him the source of disgust or berating for our failure. When we are merely human (as opposed to willfully sinful or rebellious), the heart of God towards us is pity or compassion. The frailty attendant to your basic humanity may be a source of grief or shame to you, but it is not to your Father.

All men in ministry are but men. You have had your conscience bloodied as you read a biography which focused on the great ability and untiring humanity and unflagging, burning devotion of some great saint of the past. In doing so, you've thought how unworthy a servant you are. The great servant whose biography you read was also unworthy. That saint whom God greatly blessed had, like Elijah, nature just like ours.

You need to understand your identity as a mere man. You have a limited capacity of gift, wisdom, ability, and service. You are not omnipotent nor omniscient. You do not have the power to have people embrace your counsel or to implement what you preach and teach. You need to admit that weakness to yourself and to others. You are not and cannot be a perfect pastor or a perfect husband or father. There will be times, as I have had to do repeatedly, that you confess not just the sins attendant to your calling, but the weaknesses that impact your life and ministry. There are times you have not succeeded as you desired simply because you are a man. The wayward member of the flock did not come back; the families that struggled to get along left the church; the couple with the troubled marriage divorced. Not every story is a triumph of grace. There is much we can do in ministry, but it is, in the end, only so much. We are not infinite, we are not tireless, we do not have access to the theater of everyone's conscience. God does. And when God sees that we are not God he is not angry or frustrated. He knows you are but dust—yes, glorious, articulated and Spirit indwelt dust, but dust nonetheless.

## I am in Union with Christ

The second thing you need to embrace is your identity in Christ. God does not see you first and foremost as a pastor, he sees you as his child. He sees you as one whom he set his love on before the foundation of the world. His view of you is not dependent at any given moment on how well or poorly you have performed in your office. Hopefully your sermons are consistently accurate and clear and properly illustrative and practical. Some of them will be better than others. Once or twice a year you may even preach a 'keeper.' If that sermon were a fish, you might be tempted to send it to the taxidermist. But let's be honest, most of your fish are either tossed back in the water or simply eaten and then eliminated. If your identity is wrapped up in people being in awe of your latest sermon or being transformed after an hour or two of good counsel, you are headed rapidly to a second career. There is a good reason why there are a lot of men who 'used to pastor.'

Understanding your identity in Christ is essential to pastoring in the present day. If you have access to social media, read the reviews of some brilliant new book, or attend the latest mega conference you will be tempted to compare yourself. That comparison may result in sadness, self-contempt or bitterness. I chuckled recently about a tweet I read from a couple of big time pastors who were stating how they think 'small churches of just a few hundred people is what is best.' A few hundred people? Small? I thought, 'What world do these guys live in when that's a small congregation?' I would imagine that a good number of those reading this book (as well as one of the authors) preach to less than a hundred folks, and some well under fifty. If my identity was that I was not 'successful' because I had only a few hundred people, I would be undone. My identity is not in how often I am asked to preach at other places or whether I ascend the ladder to the platform of conference speaker. It's not dependent on having a successful blog or having written a book. It's that I am a sinner who has become a saint in union with Christ. The pastor of the largest church in the world is no more the recipient of every heavenly blessing than the pastor who preaches to a dozen. The pastor whose sermons receive thousands of downloads are no more or less loved by God than the man whose years of labor will rapidly be forgotten.

## I am a Pastor

The third thing you should embrace is your identity as a pastor. We are prone to make this our chief identity. It's what we do, and it is presented in our thoughts and introductions as what we are. I do not simply pastor a church. It's not what I do, it is what I am. I do what I do because I am what I am. I am a pastor. To be a pastor, biblically speaking, means at least two things. It means first, that the Triune God has chosen you for this high and holy calling. The risen and glorified Jesus has bestowed the gift of pastor-teacher to the church (see Ephesians 4:11). Paul said of himself and his companions that they had been 'entrusted by God with the gospel.' This is an awesome, sobering, and ultimately liberating thought. I did not call nor gift myself. If I am pastoring a certain church at this time, the Sovereign King of heaven and earth has brought this about.

Secondly, being a pastor means that some local congregation has examined your life in terms of the qualifications for a pastor/elder laid out in 1 Timothy 3 and Titus 1. They have, in light of your life and gift, called you to shepherd that flock. Neither God's calling nor the congregation's approval should be the ground of boasting nor of you lording it over the flock. But they should be the grounds of confidence and hope in the midst of trouble or weariness. In a genuine biblical call, the pastor can say to God and to the flock, 'I did not seek this on my own nor did I call myself to this work or to this assembly. I'm here with a sense that Christ has given me as a gift to you, a gift you recognized and embraced.' This is something of who we are. Men in Christ called to minister. That basic understanding is crucial to our taking heed to ourselves.

## Why We Fail to Take Heed

Taking heed to ourselves is not merely an issue of understanding and embracing our humanity. It is an issue of Spirit-empowered labor guided by the precepts of divine revelation. The Bible never wastes its commands. There are no commands to breathe. Such a commandment is not needed. We are exhorted in areas of need where we have failed or are likely to neglect. Pastors must be told to watch themselves carefully because there is ever and always a temptation to neglect this vital issue. What would make a man fail to pay attention to himself? In what ways will he be tempted to neglect this clear duty in God's word?

**We're Too Busy**

The first area is a busyness rooted in service to others. You've most likely heard about a doctor somewhere who does not sleep or eat for hours as he is in the midst of caring for others in a crisis. He may say to another, 'You need to eat! You need to sleep!' And yet he carries on without these necessities. He may well be thinking he is indispensable, people will die without him, he can't take a break! Some men in ministry labor with this delusion. Others might feel this crushing weight from a demanding flock. Pastors often lament, 'I am taking heed to so many people and things that I cannot afford to consider myself.' The demands of public and private ministry (the administration of the church, crisis counseling, reaching the lost and a host of other duties) can lead us to neglect the rest and refreshment desperately needed.

It is possible to spend so much time working on healthy sermons and pursuing public and private means to aid people to grow that we fail to ensure that our own souls are fed. Paul told Timothy to remember that the hardworking farmer must partake of the crops himself—in fact, he should be the first one to feast upon the food he is cultivating for others (2 Timothy 2:6). To return to our analogy, the doctor who eats and sleeps will do more good to more patients over an extended period of time than the man who burns himself out. The pastor who does the most good to the souls of others is the one who deliberately labors to be spiritually healthy himself.

**We're Too Professional**

A second cause of failing to take heed to ourselves is a vexing form of professionalism, or what Charles Spurgeon called 'ministerialism.' Professionalism in ministry happens when a man begins to look at his Bible or prayer closet in terms of his job and not in terms of his own redeemed humanity. It's possible for the Bible—the book of books—to become for a man a textbook from which he develops sermons for others rather than a means of nourishment for his own soul. As a friend of mine has quipped, "Jeremiah did not say, 'Your word was found and I did exegete it… but 'your word was found and I ate it'"(Jeremiah 15:16)!

Spurgeon put it this way to a group of men he was training for the ministry, speaking of temptations they would battle:

> …of these the worst is the temptation to ministerialism–the tendency to read our Bibles as ministers, to pray as ministers, to get into doing the whole of our religion as not ourselves personally, but only relatively concerned with it… Brethren it is eminently hard to keep to this. Our office, instead of helping our piety, as some assert, is through the evil of our natures turned into one of its most serious hindrances; at least, I find it so.[2]

Pastors must first feed on God's word and be changed by it before we will be able to feed it to others and nurture their souls with it.

## Paying Attention to Our Spiritual Lives

If a man is to remain spiritually vigorous throughout the decades of service to Christ, he must watch over his own life. This means among other things that he must maintain a personal, loving, devotional attachment to Christ. He must embrace the same means of grace he presses his congregation to use to grow in the grace and knowledge of the Lord Jesus. A competence in systematic theology, a basic knowledge of the original languages, and creedal convictions are no substitute for this loving, personal and growing relationship with the Jesus of the Bible. Jesus can be known and, in fact, delights to be known. Paul was not a new convert nor new to the ministry when he wrote to the Philippian church that he counted all things to be loss in order that he might know Christ and the power of this resurrection (Philippians 3:9-10). To pursue that end he went to his Bible and he spent time in prayer. He gathered with God's people and enjoyed spiritual and relational fellowship with them. He set his mind on things above rather than on the things of the earth. This took conviction and effort and the help of the Holy Spirit. He pursued that knowledge for decades. After knowing Christ for years, his passion for his felt presence and desire to commune with him only deepened. His own personal experience of the unsearchable riches of Christ remained undiminished for decades.

This does not simply happen. The declension of the soul regarding our love for Christ is most often slow and imperceptible. Like the church in Ephesus, we can be busy and orthodox and seemingly prospering while our first love has drifted out of view. It is striking to see how seriously the Lord Jesus takes this issue with the church. Though they were orthodox and serious they were in danger of losing their light (which I take to be the felt presence of Christ, the very thing that makes them a true church). How did such a corporate declension take place when there were still gatherings and sermons and songs and prayers? None of those things in itself is sufficient to keep the heart warm towards Jesus.

As pastors, must commit ourselves to this relational aspect of our lives and not rely upon our professional studies. Sermon preparation is no substitute for the daily intake of the word and prayerful meditation upon that word for the good of your own soul. As of this writing I've walked with the Lord Jesus for just over 40 years. That's over 14,500 days of the Lord's mercies being new every morning. If the Lord should bless me with another 40 years, I would be looking at over 30,000 days to spend time in the word and in prayer. Anyone who has walked with the Lord will tell you that some of those days in the word are easier, better, and more delightful than others. The key is perseverance. Jesus taught that the essence of eternal life was to know God and Jesus Christ whom he had sent (John 17:3). I have long treasured the words of the prophet Jeremiah:

> Thus says the LORD: "Let not the wise man glory in his wisdom, Let not the mighty man glory in his might, Nor let the rich man glory in his riches; But let him who glories glory in this, That he understands and knows Me, That I am the LORD, exercising lovingkindness, judgment, and righteousness in the earth. For in these I delight," says the LORD.
>
> — JEREMIAH 9:23-24

As pastors there are things we are tempted to glory in. We can glory in our wisdom, the number of books we possess (whether or not we have read them, they sure look impressive in our study!), the degrees we may have attained, the conferences we have been asked to preach, the places our ministry has taken us, and of course, the size of our congregation. We may even be given over to the other temptations the text deals with. We may glory in our fitness (how much can you bench? How fast and far can you run?) and in our possessions (meager though they may be). But can we honestly glory that we both understand and know the Lord? There is overlap and distinction in these two terms. To understand the Lord is a matter of revelation. You know what God is like. If you don't know who God is and what God is like, you have no business being in ministry! But do you know him? This is the language of love and relationship. It is the language of intimacy. When Hosea is calling Israel to repentance he not only commands them to put away their idols and to return to the Lord, he urges them, 'to press on to know the LORD' (Hosea 6:1-3). The greatest commandment, after all, is to love the Lord our God with all our being.

To know someone, you must spend time with them, you must listen to them and you must speak with them. As preachers who are committed to preaching the word we will of necessity have to spend some time with the Bible. The Bible is our tool box, it is, to be crass, our 'sermon-maker.' Brothers, after years of study and preaching, is that word still precious to you? Are you asking the Lord for freshness in the midst of what can become a form a dutiful drudgery? Perhaps your soul is resisting this exhortation with charges of legalism. Ask the Lord to help you to see the word for what it is—better than the greatest of riches and more delightful than the sweetest and best foods. The Triune God with whom you fellowship is an unfathomable being of whom you know but the 'edges of his ways.'

## Paying Attention to Our Relationships

I am going to deal with this in two ways. A pastor must take heed to his family life and his life in the body. It is a given that most men in the ministry have families. The qualifications for the pastoral office in 1 Timothy 3 and Titus 1 assume this. Brian and his wife, Cara, have written a wonderful book on *The Pastor's Family*. I highly commend it to you and to your wife for careful reading.

Attaining and maintaining domestic happiness is not only a grounds for entering ministry, but a vital aspect of personal joy in and out of the church. No small part of our pastoral care will be to deal with marriages and families in need or in crisis. How are things with your own wife? Have the years taken their toll on your love and devotion to the wife of your youth? Have you allowed the demands of the pastorate to form a holy shield that allows you to neglect her? Far too many men in ministry fail to deal honestly with this area of their lives. It is easier to meet the needs of others than the needs of our own wives. We can come home emotionally and even verbally exhausted and expect her to sacrifice her enjoyment of marriage because of how much other people need us.

The specific demands of ministry never excuse neglecting the general demands of discipleship. Brothers, can you preach through the various husband passages with your wife in attendance without fearing soul crushing accusations of hypocrisy? If we are taking heed to ourselves, we must be able to demonstrate that we are not neglecting the very truths we are using to help others. I've long been fascinated by Paul's command in Colossians 3:19 for the husband to love his wife and not grow bitter towards her. How do those two things fit together? How is it that a man might grow bitter against his wife even as he seeks to love her? I think the answer lies in the fact that the duties of domestic love are difficult and unrelenting.

And what of our children? Part of taking heed to ourselves means that we take seriously the charge given to us as fathers. The sermon that must be preached and the souls that require oversight are never to be the altar upon which we sacrifice our children. To love your wife and children over the long haul is to allow your home to be a haven for yourself and for all those to whom you show hospitality. The growth and maintenance of this love will require that we take heed, that we pay close attention, that we not neglect this vital relationship.

And what of our relationship with the body? I will deal with this subject more fully in a later chapter on the role of the pastor as a churchman. What I want to emphasize at this time is the importance of paying close attention to yourself in regard to your love for the brethren you serve and with whom you fellowship and worship. Far too many men in ministry put up a relational wall of professionalism with the body of Christ. If a pastor has deep friendships, those friendships tend to exist with other men in the ministry. The congregation is a group of people we serve rather than saints in whom is all our delight. The Lord's people are not just to be seen as needy souls whom we serve with counsel and preaching, but brothers and sisters whom we dearly love. This relationship can be challenged in a host of ways. We tend to know more of the sins that beset our people. This can lead to a lack of respect and appreciation for their genuine graces. There may well be the weariness and anger that can come through those folks in the church who seem to constantly question your preaching or administration service.

Our determination to love others will always be challenged. It will be challenged by the sin and humanity of the object of our love and it will be challenged by our own sin and humanity. Are there folks in your church whom you dread seeing or hearing from? Do you know what it is to see a name pop up on your caller ID and feel a weight of disgust? We must take heed to these seeds (or full-grown plants) of bitterness, frustration, and cynicism when it comes to those who are truly precious in the sight of the Lord. Our love must be unfeigned, a love that thinks no evil, embraces no bitterness, and endures.

## Paying Attention to Our Moral Integrity

The number of pastors who have failed to watch over their moral lives is sadly legion. Pastors who are caught in their addiction to pornography, who engage in elicit actions with women, who abuse children, who wield their authority like a club, who hide their homosexuality or who steal from their congregations do incalculable harm to the church. The Gentiles blaspheme because of such things.

Whenever I am confronted with another story, especially when that story involves someone I know, I am left to ask a multitude of questions. When did it begin? How did it start? At what point did the man give in? At what point did he abandon the life-giving principle of the fear of God and make a show of his ministry? How was it possible to preach that way and profess such great truths in public when their life was privately a wreck?

Many pastors currently engage in a sinful lifestyle, and yet continue to teach and preach and give counsel. They write blogs and books. Their public theology and giftedness may seem unchanged, but the genuine blessing and anointing of the Spirit has abandoned them. They are like Samson bound with ropes who believe that once more he will arise and shake himself free as before, not realizing that the Lord has left him. These falls are, in fact, a slow descent. It did not happen all at once. They did not begin the day in the fear of the Lord and end it in the bed of another woman. They left off watching, they drifted from prayer and a hearty love for the Lord in increments. A little sleep, a little slumber, a little folding of the hands and suddenly they have so drifted from Christ that they scarce know how they got there.

The command of Solomon rings down through the centuries to guard your heart above all that you guard, for out of it flow the issues of life (Proverbs 4:23). Beware of the little sins, which, like the little foxes of the Song of Solomon, bring about great danger. Those little foxes like an extra lingering look, that seemingly innocent flirtation, checking a woman out on social media, that niggling bitterness or perceived slight, that anger over being unrecognized or unappreciated. Has your conscience slowly become eroded as you seek solace in hours of unguarded entertainment? Pastors, are you taking fire to your breast or walking on hot coals believing somehow you will not be burned and your feet will not be scorched? Are you abusing the wonders of a fully gracious salvation believing that you can sin with abandon and yet be kept in the way?

The Apostle Paul long ago warned the arrogant Corinthians stating, 'let him who thinks he stands take heed lest he fall' (1 Corinthians 10:12). In the tenth chapter of 1 Corinthians Paul leads the flock through a discussion of the sins of the wilderness generation. Like the Corinthians, Israel had enjoyed great spiritual blessings (they had been delivered from bondage, they had walked through the Red Sea, they had heard the voice of God from the mountain in the giving of the Ten Commandments) and yet they fell into idolatry and sexual sin. These things, Paul said, are recorded to help you look at yourself. They are given to be a sobering wakeup call if you are beginning to drift or compromise. Do not think that because you have sound theology and rich spiritual experiences or great giftedness or usefulness that you are exempt from watching over your heart. We must keep Solomon's warning in view that many of those who have fallen into the bed of another woman were 'mighty men.' Grace calls us to flee the first risings of sin and keeps us from embracing the lies of the enemy.

There is a place of safety where pastors and believers can walk in confidence and security. These are those who walk daily with the Lord, who live in the fear of God, and keep short accounts with God and man. Beware of the sins of bitterness and ingratitude, a selfish inward focus on how bad you have it in ministry, how God has not kept his part of the bargain or whatever it is in your life that excuses your indulgence with sin or flirtation with the world. Take heed to yourselves, dear brothers, for it is in this rigorous self-examination before our all-knowing God where we find that security, confidence and safety for our souls.

## 2

## TAKE HEED TO YOUR DOCTRINE

I assume if you are reading this book that doctrine matters to you. You may be one of those who has named your children (or your pets) after some Puritan or great preacher of the past (I actually knew a man who named his car Octavius Winslow). It may be that your love of doctrine and desire to grow deeper in theology is one of the things that convinced you to pursue the ministry. But as with any physical or mental skill, past achievement or present attainment is no guarantee of future faithfulness.

### Doctrine Matters

Our God is a God who communicates. He speaks in words and sentences and propositions. He loves truth and he hates error. He is also a God of precision. Words matter. Truth can be known, articulated, defended, and propagated. Certain doctrines throughout history rise and fall in single words or nuanced sentences. Is Jesus a god or God? Is Jesus *a* way to heaven or *the* way to the Father? What is the relation between faith and works?

Does it matter if we confuse justification with sanctification? Does it really matter if I slip into legalism or antinomianism?

Paul makes it clear that though our orthodoxy must demonstrate elements of love and humility, it must also embrace a ferocious tenacity. Paul was concerned that the body of the truth deposited to the church would be guarded by the power of the Holy Spirit and passed on, whole and intact, from one generation to another (2 Timothy 2:2). When it came to the fundamentals of the gospel, Paul would give no quarter. This is why Paul instructed Timothy to not just take heed to himself, but also to his doctrine:

> Take heed to yourself and *to the doctrine*. Continue in them, for in doing this you will save both yourself and those who hear you
>
> — EMPHASIS MINE, I TIMOTHY 4:16

Decades into his ministry he was pleading with the rising generation of preachers to take heed to their doctrine and to the careful preaching of God's word even if it were not popular.

As of the writing of this book the evangelical and Reformed camps are enjoying a time of doctrinal resurgence. When I moved to Louisville, Kentucky in 1990 the Southern Baptist Theological Seminary along with the Presbyterian seminary were liberal in their theology. That liberal doctrine affected the churches as the graduates went on to pastor. There was a time when very few would understand or care about a rich doctrinal heritage laid down in the great creeds and confessions of the church. I can remember being thrilled to hear about certain pastor's conferences where three or four hundred men might gather to hear the rich truths of God's word being proclaimed to our generation. If I had heard of a conference with over a thousand people I would have been tempted to become postmillennial. As many of you are aware, Louisville has become something of Ground Zero of a rich theological and gospel-centered resurgence. There are conferences here and elsewhere where upwards of ten thousand may gather to hear doctrinally rich expositions of God's word. The fact that we live in such a time is not a call to relax and take our armor off. Paul's exhortations to doctrinal care and conviction happened at a time when there were living apostles. If churches planted by Paul and Peter needed to guard their doctrine and if men like Timothy and Titus needed to courageously embrace the body of apostolic theology whole and intact, then we are not at liberty to slack off on our own diligence today.

## Rejecting Compromise

Paul knew that pastors would ever and always face a temptation to water down their message. It's tragic to realize that in Paul's estimation there were already 'many' who were peddling the word in his own day (2 Corinthians 2:17). There are many things that will tempt a man of God who shies away from doctrinal conviction. He may lose some of his flock through greater precision of truth or by more closely applying that truth to congregational life. If that truth is accurately, carefully, clearly, and lovingly rooted in the exegesis of the Word of God there is no guarantee that his flock will prosper (numerically or spiritually) or praise him for his love for the truth. A true shepherd will rarely be unmoved by an exodus of disgruntled people whom he loves and has committed himself to care for. No one wants to be the man who killed a church by preaching the truth to them.

In 2 Timothy 4, Paul had to remind a timid Timothy that he ultimately had to live and labor with the great day of judgment in view. He would one day stand before the Christ who is appointed to judge the living and the dead. He would not give an account to the world or to folks who did not like hearing what the Bible said about God, salvation, sin, holiness, the church or the family. There are men in ministry who will compromise or allow their mouths to be shut or their theology publicly altered to not only keep peace, but to keep their paychecks. To take heed to our doctrine is to be aware of the temptation to compromise that which Paul calls all pastors to stand firm.

## Knowing the Temptations to Compromise

There is also the great danger of changing one's theology as a result of moral compromise or societal pressure. The Bible's teaching on marriage or homosexuality or gender roles did not magically change with the evolution of society. What was common understanding and conviction a few short years ago is now considered societal blasphemy. The Bible does not change because your son or daughter is living in a certain sin. The Bible's demands for holiness are not rescinded because you yourself are failing.

Do not misunderstand what I am saying. I am not saying that your theology can never change, grow, deepen or be nuanced from where you once were. What I am saying is that such changes must not be rooted in a determination to make your church grow numerically, or to be less offensive to society, or due to personal relationships or your own failure to watch your heart. The Bible is not to be altered by us, we are to be ever and always altered by it.

We must remind ourselves that God has given us his word and that our job is to be stewards of that revelation. We are, in Paul's words, to hold fast to the pattern of sound words as we have been taught. We cannot and must not undermine the importance of sound doctrine.

## Praising 'Paint by Numbers' Preachers

We live in times when innovation is praised. Who wants to hear the same old story told in largely the same old way for thousands of years? Pastors are, in many ways, called not to be artists given liberty to paint what they like, but rather like those who have purchased a 'paint by numbers' kit. Have you seen one of these kits? A paint by numbers package comes with the drawing already made and the colors already established. Your job is to match the numbers within the lines with the paints provided. Your hope at the end of the day is to recreate the picture on the front of the box. This is our job as expositors. Not to create something new that someone will hang in a museum dedicated to our artistry, but rather tell the same story that others have told for centuries. We must remind ourselves that God has given to us a Bible that is clear regarding the most important issues of life and eternity. Who God is and how God saves and what God does when he saves people are not hard to discover if we will apply ourselves. We must remind ourselves that we hold forth a Savior who is worthy of our fidelity to his revealed truth.

When Paul told Timothy to hold fast to the truth it was in accordance with his love towards a brother in the Lord Jesus. We must remind ourselves when tempted to depart from the truth that true sheep need the exposition and application of truth to be sound and healthy. Love for the people of God should drive us to accurate exposition and God-fearing application. Some congregations may bristle at first. But if we are patient (2 Timothy 4:2), if our studies are accurate, and if we are clear, compelling, simple and loving, true sheep will begin to feed and to thrive under our preaching.

Finally, we must remember that doctrinal faithfulness is necessary for the world at-large. The very society which seems to hate the word of truth is never won over by a church's capitulation. We must give that which lost people may initially despise in order that they might be saved. The Lord is pleased to save sinners by means of the truth. That gospel which at first appears to be either foolishness or scandalous becomes the power of God to those who come to believe. Take heed to your doctrine pastors, for it will center our souls to minister this life-giving word that is the only source of truth that comforts the souls of both sheep and undershepherd.

## 3

# TAKE HEED TO YOUR FLOCK

There is a close connection between who and what we are as men and what we do in our ministry. The debate has raged over this issue in our nation in regard to our political leaders. Does it really matter what a man or woman is like in private as long as they can deliver the goods publicly? Can a piece of art be enjoyed for what it is when the artist behind that work is a reprobate of the worst sort? A doctor may be gruff, a tax cheat and an adulterer, but if he is the best at what he does I may entrust my body to his care.

But what of the pastor and his public and private labors on behalf of the church? Does it really matter if he is humble when he preaches great sermons and gives good advice? Does he have to love me in order for me to be fed by him? The specter of hypocrisy which sadly hangs over the profession of pastor is there because of the division in so many men's lives between their private and public life. All those who fall publicly have left off watching privately. As mentioned earlier, there is a close connection between our relational walk with God, our moral integrity, and our ability to teach and preach with power and fidelity. This chapter will examine the connection between our soul and our care for the flock.

## More Than a Pulpit and Study

The work of the ministry and the life of the gospel minister are, by God's design, intertwined. The shepherd lays down his life for the flock because of what he is and because of the love he bears for the flock. Who he is affects what he does. His affection for the flock drives him to self-sacrificial labor. It is sad to note, however, that many men in ministry have no real, living, vital, and affectionate relationship with the flock. The personal, private, and universal care for the flock entrusted to our watch is at the very heart of pastoral labor.

I recently heard of a local seminary student about to enter into ministry at a local church who said something to the effect, 'I'm really looking forward to preaching, but meeting with all the people is going to be annoying.' If such is the true condition of his heart, what he is saying is, 'I'm not really called to be a pastor. I want to be a preacher. I want a platform. I want people to hear and appreciate my sermons but what they do with that sermon is not my concern.' Such men want people to come to church so that he has an audience before whom he can perform. Such a man is not a pastor and quite likely is not going to be a good preacher.

When Paul told Timothy that the desire for ministry was a good thing, it was not in relation to public preaching, but in regard to private shepherding that he was speaking. Pastors are overseers, not primarily of preaching and various ministries, but of souls. We watch over souls as those who must give an account (Hebrews 13:17). What does this mean and how is this vital task to be practically carried out? What is the connection between the pastor's soul and the pastor's labor of shepherding the flock?

In 1 Peter 5:1-2 pastors are exhorted to shepherd (or tend or feed or watch) over the flock entrusted to them by the Holy Spirit. This is not an optional matter for the pastor who will give an account not only for what he preached but for how he cared for

Christ's sheep. What type of pastoral interaction is envisioned here? Is it merely that pastors should be hospitable, sociable, and friendly? Is it mere superficial and generic knowledge of the lives of the people? The Scriptures envision something far deeper. It is a shameful reality that some pastors are better acquainted with the sports or entertainment preferences members of the church enjoy than the state of their souls.

## Knowing the Flock

Does this sheep have an assurance of salvation? If not, why not? Are they reading the word? What is their prayer life like? Are they being fed by the ministry you bring? Do they feel a part of the body? How is their heart toward their brethren? Do they have confidence in you and the other leaders of the church? If the Lord of Glory were to ask you such questions about those whom he has sovereignly placed under your care, what would you say? Is it acceptable to simply shrug our shoulders and say, 'I don't have a clue,' or 'that's not my business?' If those things are on the heart of the Master, they should be on the heart of his stewards.

## Loving and Living

How does this aspect of our labor touch upon the issue of the pastor's soul? Let me give you at least two ways. The first is our heart of love towards the flock. The second is their confidence in us as men who know the word, who love them, and who are marked by a consistent godliness.

To oversee the souls of those entrusted to us we need to be able to draw near to them. We need to be motivated by a love for them that seeks their best even when it is difficult or wearying to ourselves. The Apostle Paul put it this way, 'So, affectionately longing for you, we were well pleased to impart to you not only the gospel of God, but also our own lives, because you had become dear to us' (1 Thessalonians 2:8). So too must the heart of the modern pastor be to his flock.

## Persevering in Pastoral Affections

If you are going to shepherd the same people for a long time your heart must echo that of the apostle. Love will add life and vitality to ministry that mere conviction can never bring. That one who needs your attention is not a burdensome weight to be endured, but someone precious that you love. Do the people to whom you minister know that they are dear to you? Have you made that obvious to them in your public and private interactions with them? Such love to the same flock over decades of service demands that our love be longsuffering.

I have some folks in my church whom I have pastored for nearly 30 years. One of the things that makes that possible is mutual, patient love. I have sins and quirks which will test their love. I have seen their strengths and weaknesses over the decades. Why do so few men pastor the same church for decades? Why are there so few members who walk with the same body and the same pastors for all those years? They grow weary of one another. The same offenses seen over time prove to be too much. Many pastors leave their place of ministry because they are tired of the people entrusted to them.

It is a common sin among pastors to get together and share war stories about how bad some of the people in their flock are. Like men comparing scars and how they got them, they will seek to top one another with the odd, wayward, and stubborn folks who make up their flock. Would someone listening to this group of pastors have the notion that pastoring is something that you love to do? Would they glean from your conversation that the flock is dear to you? Would you have cause for shame if the conversation was recorded and played at a congregational meeting? I know that some folks will test you. There are times when I understand why pastors move on to another church. They realize that they are exchanging one set of burdens for another but at least the burdens and those who bring them are new. We can be like men who enjoy the newly emptied septic tank. We know it will fill up again, but at least it will take a while. To truly shepherd the sheep, we must not only be convinced in our conscience by an accurate exegesis of the relevant passages, and not only equipped with a practical plan, but we must cultivate genuine love for the people of God

The subject of pastoral affections is dealt with in several key texts of Scripture. Though it is not primarily dealing with ministry, the words of Paul in 1 Corinthians 13 have a wonderful application for preachers of the word.

> Though I speak with the tongues of men and of angels, but have not love, I have become sounding brass or a clanging cymbal. And though I have the gift of prophecy, and understand all mysteries and all knowledge, and though I have all faith, so that I could remove mountains, but have not love, I am nothing. And though I bestow all my goods to feed the poor, and though I give my body to be burned, but have not love, it profits me nothing.
>
> — 1 CORINTHIANS 13:1-3

## Love Matters

Pastoral affections will enable you to endure with a degree of joy and longevity. It is obvious from Paul's epistles that churches have long been filled with difficult people. Why else would there be so many exhortations to love, forbearance, and longsuffering? Those are not words that flow from a notion of relational ease. We are to love without hypocrisy. We are to love fervently and from the heart. We are to be gracious and hopeful. Some folks are easy to love. Others, not so much. Some folks will try us simply because their personality and perspectives and convictions are so contrary to how we think. Some will test us with their general ingratitude for our ministry. There will be folks in our church who seem to believe that God has ordained them to be our great critic, picking over our sermons and questioning our general competency with a galling regularity. People will, by and large, shy away from revealing their struggles and sins if they are not confident that we care about them. God himself appeals to his people to cast their cares upon him based upon his affection for them (1 Peter 5:7). The care for our own soul and the care for the souls of others overlap again in regard to our personal integrity. To again quote the Apostle Paul in his ministry to the church in Thessalonica:

> For our gospel did not come to you in word only, but also in power, and in the Holy Spirit and in much assurance, as you know what kind of men we were among you for your sake.
>
> — 1 Thessalonians 1:5

The kind of man who can do great good to the souls of his people is the kind of man who keeps a close watch over his own life. If the folks who make up our churches are to receive the blessings and benefits of the public and private ministry of the word, it will to some degree be tied to their confidence in us as men.

In granting us access to their lives, the people of God are to some degree entrusting their shepherds with their most prized possession—their never-dying soul. Just as we do not want drunken men to fly our planes or incompetent men to operate on our children, so no churchmen will want careless men to have access to their soul.

Not only will the care for our own souls give us access to the consciences of our people, it will fuel our desire and ability to lovingly and personally interact with them over the course of our ministry. One of the great dangers of a long ministry is growing weary or cynical in our private counsel. There will be folks who will frustrate us because they do not embrace the counsel that we have given. They will frustrate us as words spoken from the pulpit or across the coffee table seem to fall upon deaf ears. There will come a time when we are tempted to ignore the clear command to 'be patient with all.' In seeking to walk closely with the God who is love and who will generously give the empowering Spirit to those who ask, we will know grace day by day to serve the Lord's people with self-denying love. Pastors, take heed to yourselves and your flock (Acts 20:28), for it is God's design to consider the souls of both shepherd and sheep together.

## 4

# TAKE HEED BECAUSE IT MATTERS

Why does all of this matter for us in ministry? Why is watching your heart, doctrine, and flock such a big deal? If we believe that our ministry is dependent upon the blessing of the Holy Spirit, if we believe that a faithful and effective ministry is more than the sum of our public gifts, administrative skills, and personal charisma we must embrace these fundamental perspectives of life and ministry. I want to close this section by offering four incentives towards keeping our hearts in ministry.

## It Matters to God

The first motivation is what I will call our Godward motivation. This should be the chief motivation of life. Whether we eat or drink or whatever we do, do all for the glory of God (1 Corinthians 10:31). When the Apostle Paul sought to motivate his apprentice, Timothy, regarding pastoral faithfulness (especially as it related to preaching), he did so by taking him to the last day, when the Lord Jesus will appear. He was reminding him that all ministry is done in the sight of God and in union with Christ.

The God before whom we will one day stand and give an account knows us altogether. This thought is gloriously liberating for some and grounds of great concern for others. Our Savior sees our hearts and desires and motivations and actions. He is the one who will one day judge the secrets of men's hearts. Were we preaching a Christ for whom we had little love and zeal? Was our great ambition to make our name known? To preach a sermon that made others think well of us? Were we building a brand, a franchise, so that people would marvel over what we did in our lives? Were we walking in private in the fear of God, or were we striving to 'do ministry' with a bad conscience?

The Apostle Paul lived in light of the judgment day. This moved him, he says, to maintain always a conscience void of offense before God and man. James tells us that double-minded and unfaithful men ought not to expect anything from the Lord, while the one who does his will is blessed (James 1:6,7; 22-25). The grace of God which brings salvation has appeared to all men and instructs us in how we should live in this present evil age (Titus 2:11-14). This is the grace to which we testify as ministers of the gospel. We are to tell sinners that grace is sufficient to cover all their sins and that having come to Christ that this same grace will liberate and empower the saved sinner to live a life that is pleasing to the Lord. This does not mean perfection, but it does mean consistent integrity.

Would you know the blessing of God and the power of the Holy Spirit upon your public and private labors? Are you living in consistent and known and unrepentant compromise? Have you convinced yourself that grace means that such rebellion does not matter? If our gospel includes the fact that Jesus is also Prophet and King, then we must testify to that truth with our careful handling of the word and the witness of our own lives. We are telling sinners that there is grace available to say no to ungodliness and worldly lusts. God knows whether or not we believe and live the message we preach to others. Our family and our flock may be fooled, but God never is.

## It Matters to Your Conscience

A second motivation in watching our hearts is the blessing that a good conscience gives to us in ministry. One of the primary marks of New Testament preaching was Spirit-wrought boldness. Boldness is marked by clarity and confidence. Boldness allows us to probe the consciences of sinners and of saints. A man who loves others can have a boldness in preaching about what love looks like. A man who has been faithful to his wife in heart and deeds can be bold in what he says, not only because he knows it is true, but because he himself has experienced the help of the Holy Spirit in this way.

There is a common saying in evangelism that we are beggars telling other beggars where we found bread. In ministry we are telling others about an experience we have had of the grace of God. We can tell sinners that we know what it is to find hope in Jesus. As saints we can testify of the warfare of the flesh lusting against the Spirit and the Spirit against the flesh. We can speak of the warfare of the believer living in a hostile world and of the schemes of the devil, not simply because we have exegeted the passages properly, but because it is the experience of our own lives. There is a great deal of difference between the sports commentator who has read all the books and the athlete who has been on the field. We can speak about places we have been and people we have met and food we have tasted and do so with far greater authority than we can if these are unknown realities to us. They may be true, but if we ourselves have not used them, then we run the risk of being a celebrity salesman pitching a product for a paycheck.

## It Matters to Your Flock

A third incentive to watching over our hearts in ministry is the effect we will have on our congregation. When Paul spoke of the transformative power of the grace of God in regard to practical godliness he told Titus to preach these things and to allow no one to despise him. Why does he say that? For good or ill people are going to consider our own lives in light of what we preach. We should recall what Jesus said about the Pharisees—do what they say, but do not according to their works for they say but they do not do. We do not want that to be said of us! If we are going to be in one place for any length of time and seek to live an open and hospitable life, those under our care will have some idea what kind of men we are.

Have you ever had a preacher whom you respected ruin his usefulness in your sight due to some interaction with him? I've heard dirty jokes, I've seen leering glances at women, I've heard excuses for sin in the lives of men in ministry. Consequently, I don't want to hear them anymore. I know what they say may be true, but I also know that on some fundamental level they don't believe it. Do you want a fat personal trainer who is dragging on a cigarette telling you to work harder while bits of glazed donuts speckle his shirt? Do you want a man who does not commune with God to talk to you about prayer, or a man who is an adulterer speaking about faithfulness? The ears and hearts of those who hear us will either shrink or enlarge due to their knowledge of our lives.

There is a story told of Ben Franklin being stopped on his way to hear the great evangelist George Whitefield. "But Mr. Franklin, you do not believe those things!" "True," he replied, "But he does." Many a flock has been made to wonder what a man really believes because of the legacy of his life.

## It Matters to The World

Finally, there is something to be said about the effect of our lives upon unbelievers. It is fascinating to note that one of the qualifications for ministry is that a man has a good reputation among outsiders. Two things are presupposed in this statement. The first is that a godly man will have some relationship with outsiders. It may be that prior to your ministry calling that you labored in secular employment or had some interaction in a social setting with those outside the faith. The second presupposition is that it matters what they think. Unbelievers may not have a great understanding of the Bible's moral teaching, but they often know enough and see enough in someone's life that they will have one of two reactions.

The first reaction is that I would never go to any church that allows a man like that to minister. If that is Christianity, then I want nothing to do with it! The second reaction is the one we desire. It happens when someone says, "I am not persuaded of the truth of Christianity, but if it produces what I see in this man's life then I can tell you that I like what I see." The observations of unbelievers have little to do with our doctrine. It has everything to do with our lives.

Therefore, pastors take heed to yourself. Take heed to your doctrine and your flock: your own soul and the souls of others are at stake.

# PART II

# PASTORAL CALL UPON A PASTOR

BRIAN CROFT

## 5

# AWAKENING

I still remember the first time I read Richard Baxter's *The Reformed Pastor*. Particularly, how surprised I was by its beginning. I was warned it was intense and I should prepare to be shocked. Then I dismissively thought, "He's writing about pastoral ministry, how shocking could it be?" Then I read the opening pages and was, needless to say, shocked.

> Take heed to yourselves, lest you be void of that saving grace of God which you offer to others, and be strangers to the effectual working of that gospel which you preach; and lest, while you proclaim to the world the necessity of a Saviour, your own hearts should neglect him and you should miss of an interest in him and his saving benefits. Take heed to yourselves, lest you perish, while you call upon others to take heed of perishing; and lest you famish yourselves while you prepare food for them... Many have warned others that they come not to that place of torment, while yet they hastened to it themselves; many a preacher is now in hell, who hath a hundred times called upon his hearers to use the utmost care and diligence to escape it.[1]

Richard Baxter lived in a day where it was common for clergy to enter church work as a secure and steady profession. One of many harmful consequences of this reality was unconverted pastors. Baxter clearly felt a deep burden to call these men to account so that their own souls might be saved, and they would not harm God's sheep as wolves posing as shepherds.

The shock for me as a young pastor was Baxter confronting me on something that is assumed in most modern evangelical circles— pastors follow Jesus. But as I personally felt Baxter confront me and question my spiritual state, I realized how much I too had assumed my gospel transformation to the point where it was not my routine to consider it. In other words, Baxter's sobering words reminded me that my approach in reading *The Reformed Pastor* reflected the way I approached the basics of the Christian life in my own life. That is, I 'have that covered,' and what I really need to focus on is growing in my ministry gifts and abilities.

It should not be assumed that pastors are converted. It should not be assumed that those that preach the gospel believe it and have been changed by it. It should not be assumed a man who earned a seminary degree and was offered a job in a church has experienced the spiritual awakening to which his theological education often referred. It should not be assumed a man who is given the office and title of a pastor is called and gifted to fulfill that office and title. This chapter will address two of the most common assumptions towards awakening in a pastor's life that are directly tied to his soul: A spiritual awakening and a pastoral awakening.

## Spiritual Awakening

There are some foundational elements that need to define the spiritual awakening of every man who would ever seek the noble work of a pastor. These things so often determine either the well-being of a pastor, or his demise. Before a man concerns himself with the task of preaching, counseling, visiting, and leading in the church as a pastor, he must first be a man who has been transformed by the power of the gospel and who walks with Jesus every day. He must see his need for Jesus and turn to him in faith. He must know Jesus and feel known by Jesus. He must love Jesus and know he is loved. He must long to experience the presence of Jesus in his daily life. He must know he is forgiven by Jesus. He must cry out to him in moments of weakness and desperation and believe he is heard. Before anything else, a pastor must be a man who is truly saved by God in Christ and walks with Jesus every day.

Second, a pastor must be a man who loves God's word. Long before a pastor would ever preach God's word, he must give himself to the study of God's word. However, knowledge is not enough. This life-giving word must create a spiritual awakening that changes the man himself. In my early twenties, I was serving as an associate pastor and was in spiritual danger. This was because I was completely unaware of my need to nurture and care for my own soul and I was not gripped by God's word. I came to a breaking point where I realized I had been entrusted to teach the teenagers of our church the Bible and I didn't know it myself. Even worse, I didn't love it like I should. Out of desperation, I asked my wife to teach me how to study the Bible. She did. God intervened in a most powerful way. The spiritual work God did in me almost overnight can only be described in this way: awakening. I would never be the same. My ministry changed. Most significantly, my understanding about my need to care for my own soul increased exponentially. As I grew in spiritual awakening through being captured by God's word, how I understood caring for God's people began to take shape.

Lastly, a pastor must love God's people. A fruit of spiritual conversion in any soul is a love for God's people. A love for God's people in the soul of a pastor doesn't magically appear with a

Master of Divinity and a sizable church salary. It comes when a man clings to Jesus as his Savior, is transformed by the word of God, and walks in it. When there is a real spiritual awakening, a pastor is able to have a genuine love for the people entrusted to him. A shepherd's love for his sheep is a simple, deep, and pure love that no one can remove. A man who experiences a true spiritual awakening that takes him from darkness to light, from bondage to sin into freedom in Christ, is the only man who can fulfill the calling of God to be his undershepherd. Baxter insisted that one should not assume this. Nor should we assume it today.

## Pastoral Awakening

Likewise to spiritual awakening, a man's pastoral calling should not be assumed. Rather, a man should carefully and intentionally evaluate his calling as a divine, awakening work that only God does. There is arguably no better work on the responsibility and the process for assessing God's calling in a man's life than the writings of Charles Bridges (1794–1869). In Bridges' book, *The Christian Ministry*, he places the responsibility for the determination of one's call upon both the conscience of the individual and the local church to which he is committed. Bridges refers to these two aspects of calling as the internal and the external call of God:

> The external call is a commission received from and recognized by the Church, not indeed qualifying the minister, but accrediting him, whom God had internally and suitably qualified. This call communicates therefore only official authority. The internal call is the voice and power of the Holy Spirit, directing the will and the judgment, and conveying personal qualifications. Both calls, however—though essentially distinct in their character and source—are indispensable for the exercise of our commission.[2]

Bridges says that an individual must receive an internal call to know he is truly called of God to serve in the ministry. This is a God-given desire to do the work of the ministry combined with his own conviction that he has been gifted and empowered by God's Spirit to do this work.

In addition to the internal call, however, an individual must also possess an external call. This is the affirmation from a local church that he possesses the gifts and godly character suitable for a Christian minister. Bridges, Charles Spurgeon, and many other godly men, whom God used in the past to prepare those called into the ministry, all agree that both the internal and external calls are necessary for a person to enter into the work.

It is this 'internal calling' that is the pastoral awakening that happens in the soul that is required for a man to be a pastor and endure throughout his ministry. This pastoral awakening can be understood by two categories: desire and qualification.

## Desire

The Apostle Paul instructs his young protégé when he writes, "It is a trustworthy statement: if any man aspires to the office of overseer [pastor], it is a fine work he desires to do" (1 Timothy 3:1). The great nineteenth century Baptist Charles Spurgeon lectured young men preparing for the ministry in this way: "The first sign of the heavenly calling is an intense, all-absorbing desire for the work."[3] There should be a strong, unquenchable desire in a man to do the work of a pastor. He should have a desire to preach God's word, shepherd God's people, evangelize the lost, disciple the spiritually immature, and serve the local church.

Spurgeon confirms that this divine aspiration which comes from above can be known through a desire to do nothing else:

If any student in this room could be content to be a newspaper editor, or a grocer, or a farmer, or a doctor, or a lawyer, or a senator, or a king, in the name of heaven and earth, let him go his way; he is not the man in whom dwells the Spirit of God in its fullness, for a man so filled with God would utterly weary of any pursuit but that for which his inmost soul pants. If on the other hand, you can say that for all the wealth of both the Indies you could not and dare not espouse any other calling so as to be put aside from preaching the gospel of Jesus Christ, then depend upon it, if other things be equally satisfactory, you have the signs of this apostleship. We must feel that woe is unto us if we preach not the gospel; the word of God must be unto us as fire in our bones, otherwise, if we undertake the ministry, we shall be unhappy in it, shall be unable to bear the self-denials incident to it, and shall be of little service to those among whom we minister.[4]

Why is an unquenchable longing for this work required? Because the work of ministry is not for the faint of heart. It is a work fraught with struggles, challenges, discouragements, pressures, and spiritual battles that can cripple the strongest of men who have an 'ordinary' desire for the work. It should, instead, be a desire that remains when your brother betrays you; a desire that is undiminished when job threats arise; a desire that endures when physical, mental, and emotional fatigue firmly take root. And it is a desire that should increase over time. This desire is a primary evidence of the divine call of a pastoral awakening.

## Qualification

Many faithful, godly men throughout the ages have displayed Christ in their character and have modeled sacrificial service to his church. Yet not all have been called to the work of pastor/elder.

Paul writes to Timothy and he gives a separate list of qualifications for the office of pastor/elder, distinct from deacons (1 Timothy 3:8-13). This list demonstrates that there is a unique calling and work that a pastor is set apart to do. These qualifications provide a way for others to evaluate externally and objectively a man who claims to have a desire for this work. Paul's list of qualifications for the office of the pastor can be summarized into five categories:

## Able to Teach

The ability to teach is the primary qualification that sets apart the work of a pastor from all others in the church. Paul writes that a man must be *able to teach* (1 Timothy 3:2). This qualification refers to more than just a desire to teach. It involves having the skill and ability to teach God's word faithfully, accurately, and effectively. Paul confirms this elsewhere when he says that God has entrusted these men to "guard, through the Holy Spirit who dwells in us, the treasure" of the gospel (2 Timothy 1:14).

This requirement for being able to teach should also be understood in light of what James writes about teachers. James warns that there is a "stricter judgment" for those who teach in the church (James 3:1). Those who have been gifted by God for this task should teach humbly, clearly, passionately, and faithfully. The call to teach involves preaching the word (2 Timothy 4:2) whatever the cost, seizing every opportunity to make the gospel clear by presenting the treasure and value of Christ, calling people to repent and believe, and then trusting in the power of the Holy Spirit to transform hearts and minds. The ability to instruct God's people with his word is referred to as "reproving, rebuking, and exhorting" (2 Timothy 4:2), and it should define gospel ministry, both public and private. As Roger Ellsworth has rightly observed, "Fail here and you would have failed in your central task."[5]

## A Blameless Reputation

Paul's command that a pastor "must be above reproach" (1 Timothy 3:2) is listed to emphasize that he should not just flee from evil, but should seek to avoid even the *appearance* of evil. For example, it is hard to accuse a pastor of having an affair if everyone knows that a pastor will not be alone in a room with another woman other than his wife. The qualification to have a blameless reputation means that a pastor should seek to live in a way that avoids accusations. He should seek to live a consistent, godly life and cultivate a good reputation among all people. Not being in bondage to any substance, but being self-controlled affirms this reputation, which seems to be why Paul also mentions that he should not be "addicted to wine" (1 Timothy 3:3).

Having a blameless reputation also involves having a "good reputation with those outside the church, so that he may not fall into reproach and the snare of the devil" (1 Timothy 3:7). This does not mean backing down from the truth or trying to compromise with the world; it means living in a way that demonstrates God's love and compassion for the lost, that they will "on account of your good deeds, as they observe them, glorify God in the day of visitation" (1 Peter 2:12).

## Manages his Family

A third qualification for the call to be a pastor is to be "the husband of one wife" (1 Timothy 3:2). This phrase is commonly misunderstood to mean that a pastor must be married and cannot be single, but the phrase is not referring to marital status. It refers to faithfulness—that a man is committed and faithful to his one wife. A pastor's leadership in the home is shown by the depth of his love for his wife, living sacrificially "just as Christ also loved the church and gave Himself up for her" (Ephesians 5:25). This command is given to all Christian men to love their wives in this way, but a pastor is called to model this for his people.

This qualification, when taken together with Paul's additional instructions to Timothy, also indicates that a woman is not to exercise authority over a man (1 Timothy 2:12). Just as men are to lead their families, God's design is for the men to lead the church.

This principle also applies to children living in a pastor's home. A pastor is to shepherd, teach, care, and manage his children faithfully (1 Timothy 3:4). This does not require that a pastor must have children or that his children must necessarily be converted. It means that a pastor's children must respect his authority as the God-appointed head and leader of the family. Why does this matter? Paul gives a very profound reason: "For if a man does not know how to manage his own household, how will he take care of the church of God?" (1 Timothy 3:5).

Along with managing his household, a pastor should also be warm and welcoming toward outsiders and visitors to his home. He should be "hospitable" (1 Timothy 3:2). Most people only think of this as welcoming people into their home—and that is certainly true—but hospitality more generally speaks of your disposition and attitude toward strangers. It's not difficult to be hospitable to people you know and love, but few of us are hospitable to strangers we don't know. Paul tells us that a pastor should model a willingness to care for others—even those he does not know. He also implies that he should train his household to embrace this as a calling for the entire family.

### Godly Character

Most of the characteristics Paul lists could be lumped into the general category of godly character. Paul tells us that a pastor is to be "temperate, prudent, and respectable" (1 Timothy 3:2) as well as "gentle and not contentious" (1 Timothy 3:3). All of these qualities speak of the inward transformation of the gospel, how Christ is reflected in a person as they are kind, compassionate, self-controlled with words and actions, honorable, humble, and full of discernment and wisdom. It is difficult to overstate the importance of this as a requirement for leadership and ministry. It is no accident that most of Paul's qualifications for pastoral ministry fall into this category of godly character. Those who desire the work of pastoral ministry should labor diligently to grow in these qualities, knowing that it is the grace of God and the transforming power of the gospel that empowers their growth.

## Spiritual Maturity

Many of these qualities also point to the requirement of spiritual maturity, but I think there are two qualities in particular that indicate this. First, Paul tells us that a pastor is to be "free from the love of money" (1 Timothy 3:3). A pastor's primary responsibility is to preach and teach the word of God and sacrificially care for his people—not to seek financial gain for himself. Assessing if a person is free of the love of money is not about how much money a pastor has or what he will get paid; it is about what the pastor does with the money he has. Having a love for money speaks of a desire to have more and more of it. A pastor should be compensated for the work he does, but a man should not enter the ministry out of a desire for personal material gain.

Secondly, as the spiritual leaders and doctrinal gatekeepers of the church, pastors cannot be "new converts" (1 Timothy 3:6). This means that a spiritually immature person should not enter this work. This makes sense for obvious reasons, but in the text Paul gives a specific one—"lest he become conceited and fall into the condemnation incurred by the devil" (1 Timothy 3:6). An immature believer could easily get caught up in the power of the position instead of seeing the office as a sacrifice and service to God and his people. Pursuing pastoral ministry also places a man on the front line of spiritual attack from the enemy, which seems to be one of the several reasons the New Testament calls for a plurality of godly, spiritually mature pastors/elders in a local church. Multiple pastors and elders in leadership allows for greater accountability and fellowship, and the church to benefits from their accumulated wisdom (Titus 1:5; Acts 20:28; 1 Peter 5:1).

Whether a spiritual or pastoral awakening, they both come from the power of God as his Spirit is mightily at work in a man's soul. One should never assume these. They are both a work of God, not man. Although both are an internal work of the Holy Spirit, they both should be visible to others. Therefore, they are both a God-ordained work in the soul that must serve as the foundation for a pastor's labors and ability to care for his own soul.

# 6

## STRENGTH

There's something you should know. I am weak. The problem is, I don't like being weak. I was taught growing up that it was bad to be weak; it was pathetic to be needy. Weakness brought pain in my life. As a result, I have spent most of my life fighting against weakness. This way of living is devastating to a man's soul. It was to mine. In an effort to hide the weakness of my life, I performed in such a way that I looked strong to those around me. After a while, I was even able to deceive myself that the weakness had fled. And yet, my soul was dying inside. One of the best ways to crush your own soul is to know deep down inside you are human, weak, needy, frail, and that God has made you this way, but you still reject it. At this stage, we are no longer fighting against the presence of weakness in our life, but the design of a good and perfect Creator and the effects of sin on that design. No wonder we lose this battle and the soul of a man is crushed.

When pastors live this way, the results can be even more devastating. In addition to the regular pressures of life, pastors face this reality of their weakness in front of their congregations who look to them to see how they face their own frailty and weakness.

How a pastor approaches dealing with weakness in his own life will not only affect his own soul, but will directly affect the lives of those who seek his care and look to make sense of their own weakness. Many souls are inevitably affected. First and foremost is the soul of the pastor.

The reality is that God calls pastors to be strong and courageous. But how should we make sense of strength and courage? Pastors are commonly pressured to have it all together, to have it all figured out, and therefore are assumed to be the experts to instruct everyone else on how to do life. The biblical qualifications that are to reflect spiritual maturity and being above reproach can easily slide into this unachievable perfectionistic standard that prevents many pastors from being themselves before their people. However, God calls a pastor to step up and be courageous in this way: Show up as weak and needy before the church you pastor. This chapter aims to help pastors embrace their weakness as God calls us to do—this cannot be done without engaging the soul. God calls us to embrace our weakness, and in doing so, we find divine strength and courage.

Do not underestimate the power of God to bring fruit and life into a church when a pastor lives a transparent, authentic life before God's people. The reality is that pastors are just as weak and needy as everyone else in the church. Pastors need to embrace this calling to live an honest, authentic life before their people. Let them see you struggle. Let them know you are hurting. Remind them you are not perfect and are not in control. The most courageous pastors are the ones who don't perform, but rest in their identity in Christ and live in the freedom of being themselves before their people.

## Strength in weakness

The idea of strength in weakness sounds like an opposing idea. Many would say you cannot be strong and weak at the same time. But the Bible gives a very different understanding, captured most clearly in a letter Paul wrote to the Corinthians when he referred to his request of God to remove a thorn in his flesh and God responds:

> My grace is sufficient for you for power is perfected in weakness. Most gladly then I will rather boast about my weaknesses so that the power of Christ may dwell in me. Therefore, I am well content with weaknesses, with insults, with difficulties...for Christ's sake; for when I am weak, then I am strong.
>
> — 2 CORINTHIANS 12:9-10

I have a confession to make. I would have always affirmed Paul's teaching here as true. But I have spent most of my life living as if strength in weakness cannot co-exist. However, I am learning this is the key to understanding how to live courageously and in the freedom of the gospel. True strength comes from Jesus living in us and that is most magnified when we are weak and needy for him. This is soul work. Christ's presence is most cultivated in us when we embrace the reality of our weakness, sinfulness, and humanity. In Christ, we find true strength, not despite our weakness, *but in our weakness*. A courageous pastor embraces his weakness and finds divine strength.

## Walking in weakness

Shifting this idea of true biblical strength will bring this natural question, "How does a pastor own his weakness and humanity and gain this gospel-empowering strength?" Consider these three realities of weakness that, if embraced by pastors, will produce gospel-empowering strength:

## Pastors must embrace that we are all sinners.

It is essential to embrace our humanity and the things that make us human. The truth that "God is God and you are not" should be a precious, freeing truth to our souls. If we are human, we are sinners. We will sin. This is the reason we all need Jesus. This is not a call to embrace sin. But we do need to embrace that we are sinners who will struggle with sin. Ironically, a problem many pastors possess that saps our strength is that we are frustrated that we are sinners. We preach for sinners to turn to Jesus, all the while irritated with the reality we are sinners also. A common challenge to pastors is that our own people struggle to accept us as broken sinners. The pressure to perform for our people is immense. It is a pressure that is sometimes imposed by our people, while other times self-inflicted. But this is the heart of the gospel we preach. This is why we need Jesus. If we are unable to embrace who we are in our fallen state and our need for Jesus in that, we will not receive fully God's grace as we ought. We will not walk in the freedom that forgiveness brings. We will not be equipped to lead our people to that river of grace. And our souls will crumble.

## Pastors must embrace that none are perfect.

Pastors love to declare the sinlessness of Jesus and that only Jesus is perfect, yet these same pastors are crippled by a fear of failure. Pastors are devastated because they do not measure up to the expectations they set for themselves and others set for them. I have news for you. We are not perfect. We can't and won't do everything right. We will fail. Guess what? That is okay. God has already accepted us. We are clothed in Christ's righteousness. We must check those expectations we place on ourselves. All pastors are painfully aware of the high expectations our churches place on us. However, they usually pale in comparison to the ridiculous expectations we place on ourselves. Are you crushing yourself under the weight of perfectionism? Perfectionism is not a virtue, as many like to believe. It is a sin, in which we try to be like God. It is a declaration that we think we can achieve perfection, so we strive for it. But we crush our souls in the process. Only God is perfect. Perfectionism has been a strength killer for years in my life. It has been so freeing in the last several years to embrace this weakness— you should too, for the sake of your soul.

### Pastors must embrace their physical frailties.

In part four of this book we will be digging into the specifics of how to physically care for ourselves in such a way that directly affects our souls. Let's prime the pump by considering how much you embrace the reality of your physical humanity. Pastors love to be the ones who appear super-human and unaffected by the realities of the fall on our bodies. So, we determine the amount of sleep we get around what needs to be done, not how much sleep we need. We eat what we want and dismiss it as fuel for this noble task in which we labor—despite gaining ten pounds each year. We avoid exercise out of time constraints, or we exercise regularly, but ignore the most recent injury that is telling us to rest. We ignore the warning signs of stress, depression, and anxiety that the body so often communicates to us if we listen. We keep pressing on and pressing through—until we hit the wall. Part of embracing our weakness is to be smart and wise about our physical limitations; to know when to run and go and know when to stop and rest.

I hit that wall about five years ago. It was in a season where my ministry in all areas was flourishing. But my soul was dying. My marriage was struggling. My wife was in a dark place. I had run our family into the ground. So much of the mental and emotional breakdown I experienced was rooted in the build-up of this pressure of rejecting my weakness and humanity and the fear of facing it. It took me almost losing it all for me to get help. Even then I did it begrudgingly. God used a very wise and skilled counselor and some close, patient pastoral friends to take me on a journey long-needed. It was a very painful journey that shook my identity to the core that began with seeing the reality of my weakness. It was a journey to understand and embrace my weakness and trusting Jesus would meet me there—and give me strength. He did. I am still on this journey, but my life is radically different. My soul is at peace in a way I never thought possible. I have experienced first-hand that in Christ, there is indeed strength when we embrace our weakness.

Embrace your weakness dear brothers and fellow pastors. Only the redemptive power of Christ at work in us can take our weakness and make us strong. Courage through true strength comes not despite our weakness, but because of it.

# 7
---
## LOVE

Most of us are very familiar with the stoic, tough guy masculinity that is taught to boys as they grow up. In its best form it is designed to produce hard-working, dependable, stable men who will support their family, contribute to society, and persevere through adversity. And yet, many in the world are puzzled that the highest rates of suicide come from men, those who have been trained to be tough and unshakable. Here's how one secular writer tries to make sense of this inconsistency:

> Men are dying, dying in great numbers. It's a massive tragedy and it's going on under our noses, in our countries, our cities, our suburbs and in our neighborhoods. We know from previous data that predominantly it is men taking their own lives, but what we don't tackle with enough willingness are the depths of the reasons why. It's not necessarily simple but a great start would be if we were to stop championing the aggressive, stoical form of masculinity that is embedded in society.[1]

It is safe to say all men have been affected by this worldly version of masculinity where real men don't cry. Real men are tough, stoic, unshakable, unmovable, self-reliant. Nothing is to rattle a man, and if it does it is considered a sign of a weak man. What boy wasn't told after skinning his knee while playing in a game that he should rub some dirt on it and get back in there? What young man hasn't fought back tears when wounded out of fear of what his buddies might think? Whether a man's own father taught this type of masculinity or it was captured on the big screen, it is deeply embedded into the culture of which we live. This type of tough guy pressure men feel has ramifications other than the horrific reality of suicide for a few. The even greater tragedy is the way this form of masculinity paralyzes so many men's ability to love another person.

This false masculinity exists in the church also. Many churches and seminaries articulate a vision for biblical manhood that only emphasizes one half of the full biblical picture. This flag of manhood waved portrays a hunting, flannel-wearing, steak-eating, tough guy who shoots guns—and likes it! To them, biblical manhood is only about initiative, leadership, and grit, which are all wonderful qualities in a Christian man. However, this singular focus leads to the neglect of a fuller understanding of biblical manhood that includes tenderness, compassion, and love.

How should Christians process this type of masculinity, especially pastors? Here's a bold statement about this type of masculinity that should inform our evaluation. It is a lie. It is unbiblical. There is no evidence in the New Testament that Jesus was stoic and unshakable. Quite the opposite. It is an unfulfilling way to live life. It hinders a man's ability to feel love and compassion for hurting people. If I'm right, what happens to a pastor who embraces this worldly masculinity, yet has a unique calling emotionally and relationally to connect with hurting people? He is, at the least, ineffective, and many times harms hurting people more. The pastoral call is to deeply love out of our own humanity and weakness. This cannot happen until the presuppositions we carry about being a "real man" get challenged at the soul level. It is the health of our souls that enables us to love others. This chapter seeks to help pastors confront this wrongheaded view of masculinity the world has sold us, present a more biblical understanding of it, then help pastors begin to evaluate their own souls in their capacity to love.

## Feel Deeply to Love Deeply

God created us with emotions. They are a part of being created in his image (Genesis 1:27). There is something important about our emotions we need to remember. We cannot suppress emotion out of fear and then assume we can somehow still feel deeply. Part of our call to be effective shepherds is rooted in allowing ourselves to feel emotion and not be afraid of it. It's good to cry and feel sadness. It's good to allow yourself to feel anger. It's good to allow yourself to feel fear. It's good to allow yourself to feel hurt and frustrated. Our emotions remind us of our humanity and that Jesus had emotions also.

Jesus felt deeply. Jesus felt righteous anger when he cleansed the temple (Matthew 21:12). Jesus experienced deep sadness when he wept at the tomb of Lazarus (John 11:35). Jesus endured fear and anguish as he prayed in the Garden of Gethsemane (Luke 22:44). The Chief Shepherd feels deeply. So too are his undershepherds to feel deeply. God made our emotions to help us feel deeply to be the gateway to gaze into our souls. It is through our emotions that we grow aware of the activity in our souls and learn how to love deeply.

And yet, a caution is needed as we allow ourselves to feel deeply. Paul instructs all believers to be angry and do not sin (Ephesians 4:26). Paul writes to his young protégé Timothy that although we will experience real feelings of fear, God did not give us a spirit of fear (2 Timothy 1:7). Thus, it is also important we are aware of the struggle with sin that can manifest in these emotions that should not be ignored. Nevertheless, pastors are called to feel deeply so we are able to love deeply. The tough, unshakable, stoic cannot love deeply. Paul has advocated how Christians are to love deeply and sacrificially (1 Corinthians 13). A courageous pastor loves deeply as he risks feeling deeply.

## A Love Test

The intent of most pastors is to love deeply and sacrificially, but many are not aware if that love transfers to others. This kind of love requires deep soul work that relies on the Spirit of God. It can be hard for anyone to know how to grow aware of the activity of the soul in regard to this work. Here are a couple of ways to test your soul's awareness and ability to love.

## Test #1: Do you allow yourself to feel deep emotion?

There are many reasons that could keep a person from feeling deeply. Here are a few most common examples I often experience with both men and women. First is the man who was taught all emotion is bad and it is unmanly to show it. He was taught emotion makes you less of a man and less of a person. It will give you the appearance of being weak and incapable. Second is the woman who was told she's too emotional, which made emotion bad. So, this woman was told to deal with this "problem" by doing whatever she must to control it. Lastly, many people experienced such horrible trauma in their lives such as abuse that causes them to be afraid to feel deeply because the pain of those experiences is too much. In every case, it causes individuals to go throughout their life believing a lie—emotion is bad. This does not magically change in a man's life when he finishes seminary and is handed the title of Senior Pastor.

The gospel of Jesus Christ can bring healing to our souls in such a way that in our new resurrected self we are able to feel deeply and care selflessly for others. A restored ability to feel is one of many areas where the power of Christ through the Holy Spirit can take root in our souls and change us. It is in our weakness that the power of Christ is perfected (2 Corinthians 12:9). Embrace the gift of feeling deeply and if there is something keeping you from being able to do this, begin to face it knowing Jesus can heal the most wounded, suppressed heart. Allow other trusted pastors in your life to help you find healing in these areas of your life that may be crushing your ability to feel deeply.

## Test # 2: Are you able to experience compassion for hurting people?

It is an all too common mistake to confuse understanding with compassion. I assure you, there is a difference—experienced especially in the person on the receiving end. Mental acknowledgement recognizes a person is hurting and even sees a justified reason they hurt. But there remains a disconnect to empathize, to carry the burden and feel the hurt with them. Compassion on the other hand allows another human being to empathize—to share the feelings of another. They don't simply acknowledge the hurt but experience the hurt with them. They truly bear the burden with them (Galatians 6:2). Herein marks a crucial difference in the human experience. How we engage with hurting people communicates with our words, our posture, our tone, our eye contact whether we simply understand, or actually empathize and bear the burden with them. Compassion allows a pastor to love and feel for the hurting person more deeply and genuinely.

Churches don't simply need pastors. This unique work requires courageous pastors. Men who are so secure in their identity in Christ that they are able to embrace their humanity, frailty, sin, weakness, and failures and remember they are loved and accepted by Jesus because of the gospel. This kind of pastor shows up as a compassionate pastor; a humble and teachable pastor; a wise and discerning pastor able to assess the activity of his own soul and the souls of others. Pastors don't need to be perfect or have it all together. They simply need Jesus and know they need Jesus just as badly as everyone else. It is a courageous pastor who finds his strength in his weakness and deeply loves in such a way that he is able to care well for his own soul and the souls under his care. May God give pastors the grace needed to serve hurting churches in this way not just for the sake of Christ's church, but also to preserve the soul of the pastor doing this noble work for God's glory.

# PART III

## SPIRITUAL CARE OF A PASTOR

JIM SAVASTIO

# 8

# RECEIVING THE PUBLIC MEANS OF GRACE

Over the years I have enjoyed being a part of various communities away from my church. I am thinking of things like the baseball families or the world of theater that I became part of as a parent. In these places I was not "Pastor Jim" but simply "Jim" or my kid's dad. I enjoyed these brief respites from the constant burden of shepherding. There are times when I have longed to be a part of my church simply as a member. I long to relate to brothers and sisters as another brother and not as their pastor. Sometimes this desire has been rooted in my own personal convictions of the nature of church membership. I've wanted to find a means of demonstrating that much of what I do in relation to the church is because I am a Christian and not because I am a pastor. It's easy for folks to think that the reason a pastor is faithful in his attendance and faithful in his hospitality is because it's his job. Sometimes the thought might be, "Of course he goes to prayer meeting; he's paid to go." I do not gather with the body, pray, fellowship, and open my home preeminently because I am a pastor but because I am a Christian. I do so because I am convinced it is my duty and delight as a child of

God to do so. This distinction may not be clear in the eyes of your church, but it ought to be clear in your own heart and soul.

## Just Some Guy from The Church

Is it possible to relate to the church apart from your identity as the pastor? Is it possible to enjoy the blessings and benefits of church membership in ways that are not related to public and private ministry? I caught a wonderful glimpse of this possibility during a recent trip to the hospital. Winston, a seven-year-old from the church, was going into surgery on his hand due to an infection he received when a cat bit him. Shortly before he was to be wheeled back for surgery I entered into the little cubicle to pray with him and his parents. When the attending nurse saw me she asked the little boy, "Winston, do you know who this man is?" He sheepishly replied, "Yes." "Well," she said, "Who is he?" The boy said, "He's just some guy from my church." I loved it. That's really what I want to be—just some guy from the church. Yes, I preach and teach and lead prayer times and do counseling. I am thankful for someone, even if they are seven, who can see me clearly for what I am. Not first and foremost one of the pastors, not the "Big Pastor" who has carried the bulk of public ministry for nearly 30 years, but just some guy from the church.

## Believing What We Tell Others

If you are in ministry you ought to be convinced that your calling is a high and holy one. You should also be convinced that the church is central to God's plan on the earth. However despised and lowly the church may be in the sight of the world, it is the bride of Christ and the apple of his eye. The church has a glorious identity. To be part of the church is to be part of his body, the fullness of him who fills all in all. To be part of the church is to be a member of the household of God, the New Covenant Temple indwelt by the Holy Spirit. To be a member of a church means that I am part of the house of the living God, which is the pillar and ground of the truth. Jesus loved the church and gave himself up for her. He loves and nourishes the church and will one day present her to himself without spot or wrinkle or any such thing.

The church also has a glorious purpose in the world. It is the church that has been given the commission by the risen Jesus to preach the gospel to the nations, to disciple believers, to plant churches, and to shine in such a way that our Father in heaven is glorified. The church has a glorious destination. One day the church will inherit the earth. Those who make up the body of Christ will be raised in perfection. The church will be forever with the Lord. These blessings and promises do not come to us because we lead the church or preach to the church or serve the church. They belong to us because we are in Christ and hence a part of his body and bride.

Would these convictions be as sharp and compelling if you were out of the ministry? I've born witness to the sight of men who once had high and lofty words about the preciousness and importance of the church while they were pastoring. Once they left the ministry however, their "theology" underwent a shocking decline. Is preaching precious and necessary if you never utter another word in public? Are times of corporate worship and prayer glorious to you when you don't lead them? Are the saints your delight, leaving aside that you are tasked with caring for them and compensated in that endeavor? Embracing the public means of grace for all will make us more faithful shepherds.

## More Than Shepherds

As pastors we proclaim with gusto the importance of the local church, the value of preaching, and the great blessing of having godly gifted men oversee your soul. If we are aware of a professing believer who is not a part of a church we most likely look for an opportunity to rebuke them or exhort them regarding how important it is for believers to partake of the public means of grace. For all this truth and conviction there is often a problem with men in the ministry. The problem is that men in ministry do not personally partake of the blessings that they impress upon others. What do I mean?

Many pastors reading this book will be in a place of primary leadership and in some cases, exclusive leadership. If you have fellow pastors, you may be the Senior Pastor or primary teaching and preaching elder. What that can mean is that almost all the preaching you hear is your own. And it can be the case that you listen to other preachers in your church as a mentor, listening for ways to be helpful to the preacher rather than as a simple disciple gratefully taking in the nourishment of God's word. If we are in ministry we know what it is to look for folks who are hurting or who need encouragement. We constantly keep our eyes open for hurting or needy people. We place phone calls or send texts or set up meetings to come alongside those who are weak and struggling. We give and we give and we give but rarely do we take in. When was the last time you received a call from a brother or from one of your elders to see how you are doing? When was the last time someone asked you how it is with your own soul? When was the last time a brother in the church drew near to offer encouragement or had access to our conscience in regard to some struggle?

Our flock and fellow elders may think that we do not need a pastor in the way that the "average sheep" does. Is this conclusion something that they have reached on their own or is it something that we have cultivated? Have we had the thought that the best way to be helpful to others is to be opaque? Do we have the idea that if the people of God knew that we were weary or discouraged or at times depressed that they could no longer receive spiritual nourishment from us?

If folks do not view us as needy sheep we may well be reaping what we have sown. We may give to others the thought that we are safe behind the wall of professional ministry. "My heart is just fine, thank you very much." Our walk with God is always sweet. Our minds are always on things above. We breath the air of perpetual incense as we labor in the temple of our study. We never struggle with our wives, we have no problems with our children—until we do. This is a soul-crushing way for a pastor to live and it will not last.

## I Need a Pastor and I Need a Church

We may begin to believe this lie ourselves. Others need the church. Others need us, but we do not need them. We would go after the conscience of a professing believer who says that they can serve Christ in isolation from the body. We would decry a Christian who said that they did not need to have men preach to them or care for their souls. We would tell them clearly that the Bible says otherwise. The church and pastoral ministry exist not only for the glory of God but because all Christians living in this present age need them to exist.

Christians need to be present in the worship of God every week. They need a man of God to open the Word of God to their needy souls every week. They need not only faithful brethren but skilled shepherds to check on them to help them outside of the pulpit. If this rings true to you regarding those under your care, then realize that it is true of you as well. Before you are a pastor you are a Christian.

To put it simply: shepherds are sheep first. Do sheep need shepherds and overseers of their souls? Then so do you. Do believers need the fellowship of God's people to survive in this world? Then so do you. Do believers need to sit in the flock and receive the public means of grace? Then so do you. The man of God who gives the word must also be a recipient of that word. The one who serves at the table also needs the nourishment of that communion. If you embrace the Bible's high appreciation for what preaching is and does, then it is necessary that we ourselves partake of that blessing from someone other than ourselves. That means that you must find a way for others to minister to you. That means finding a way to regularly have the word preached to your own soul as a child of God.

## We Need a Plan

There are a variety of ways in which this can take place. You may be in a smaller congregation where you do not have much help in the pulpit. Out of necessity, you will do the bulk of the preaching. Here are two ways to seek help so that you can embrace more readily these means of grace.

First, seek to find gifted men who can preach in your flock. Are there men whose gifts you can help to cultivate who may take some public teaching or preaching at least a couple of times a month that will allow you to sit as a worshiper with your family? It is good for you from time to time to allow others to lead the service, to partake of the benefit of the word being publicly read, of having others lead the singing or the serving of the Lord's table. It may be someone who is not as gifted as you to minister the word. However, look for competent men who will be faithful to fill in for you.

Secondly, develop friendships with other pastors in the area. If that pastor has fellow elders, he or one of his co-laborers might be able to come among you with some regularity to preach and teach. This is not so much because you need a "break" as it is that you need the preaching of the word yourself. Explain this to your congregation. Let them know that if you are to give you must also receive. If neither of these options are currently available to you, I would urge you at the very least to take advantage of recorded or printed sermons from gifted men whose insights into the word penetrate your soul.

The public means of grace exists as God's design for every Christian for the good of the soul. It's why they are called, "means of grace." God uniquely ministers grace through them. Pastors are no different. We need them. Our souls long for them. Receive them knowing they are God's way of ministering grace to the weary soul of a pastor.

# 9

# EMBRACING THE PRIVATE MEANS OF GRACE

The matter of maintaining spiritual vitality through the private intake of the word, mediation, and prayer has already been dealt with to some degree in a previous chapter. I don't know a single pastor who would not be alarmed to hear that a member of their church is living in daily neglect of the means that God has provided for their spiritual sustenance and vigor. The man who knows God's blessing on his life meditates on the law of God day and night (Psalm 1) and has scheduled times to bring their heart before God in prayer. It should be equally alarming to find this neglect in a man called to ministry.

This chapter spends some time developing this theme with particular reference to our calling. In our public and private ministry, we are calling people to both knowledge and experience. We are not simply telling people who God is and what God has done and said. We are not simply expounding and applying the Lord's will for our lives. We are exhorting people to know the Lord. We are exhorting people to an experience not just of conversion but of actually walking with and communing with the one true and living God. In conversion we come to know God. As pastors we have both great blessings as well as unique dangers in this aspect of the Christian life.

Many pastors enjoy the great blessing and benefit of laboring full time in the word and in prayer. This means that your church has given generously enough that you can give all your working hours to eternal things. I've often had someone say after a sermon, "I can't believe how much you got out of that text!" I will often reply, "Well, I had forty or fifty hours this week to meditate upon it and study it!" Imagine, it's our job to study the Bible! It's our job to wade through the unsearchable riches of Christ and then to present his truth to his people week after week. It's our great privilege to come to the broken-hearted or the confused with the hope and light of God's word. It's our job to go after wayward sheep and be the mouthpiece of the Great Shepherd. We have time to pray, time to read commentaries, time to read or listen to sermons, go to chapel services, and have meals with folks in which the conversation is often directly spiritual. How is this anything other than wonderful?

The previous chapter addressed the issue of professionalism or the temptation to read the Bible as a preacher, interacting with it as though we were going to expound it for the congregation rather than seeing ourselves as believers in need of simple nourishment and communion with God. There is another concern that we must keep in mind. That is, allowing the profoundly beautiful to become mundane. Few things are harder to maintain in life than a sense of wonder and awe.

## Avoiding Park Ranger Syndrome

Last year I had the privilege of taking my wife and children to the Grand Canyon. This trip had been talked about for almost twenty years. What finally made us take the trip was that my daughter, Olivia, was getting married in the next few months. This was the last time we would all be together in this way. If you have ever been to the Canyon you know that pictures, videos, and descriptions of others cannot do it justice. You have to see it for yourself. Hundreds of thousands of people from all over the world make the drive into the park and stare in silent wonder at the vastness and beauty of this part of God's creation. But not everyone who comes to the Canyon is a visitor. Some of those standing around are the men and women who work at the national park. Some of them are park rangers who have studied the Canyon and the history of the park. It's their job to be there every day. They get to tell eager people about the wonderful sight before them. They get to see eyes light up and witness the jaws dropping at what is presented to them. They no doubt know that they have a cool job and that what they represent is truly great. However, after a period of months, or certainly years, that Canyon can become, emotionally speaking, a simple hole in the ground. How can it retain its emotional grandeur after seeing it a thousand times?

To change the analogy, think of the first time you touched your wife's hand or the first time you saw your firstborn child. I used to stare at my daughter as she slept. Her every movement as a newborn had some emotional impact on me. Well, twenty-six years later that is no longer the case. I am not tempted to take a thousand pictures of her doing things. I don't feel the electric shock shuddering through my body when I kiss my wife. Time and repetition has eroded the felt sensations. The key is to keep hungry and stay needy.

## Keeping Hungry

How then can we retain a hunger and thirst for God's word. How do we come to it over and over again with the felt sense of what the Bible is? This is especially true for us as pastors to experience. Most believers spend very little time in their Bible in a given week. The most dedicated of disciples may spend upwards of an hour studying its riches. But it is our job to spend hours in study, analysis, and meditation. It is possible for great things to become common. It is possible that we can teach a truth that used to cause our souls to well up with worship, but now find our emotions disengaged. Our great familiarity with the word can become, if we are not careful, the means of emotionally and spiritually distancing ourselves from the word. Sadly, it's possible that we can know the content of our Bibles better and yet know our God less. It is crucial that we keep hungry for God and for his word and long for it to feed our own souls.

## Staying Needy

And what of prayer? If you want to make virtually any believer feel inadequate, ask him about his prayer life. Many pastors will readily confess that it is far easier to labor in the word than it is to devote themselves to prayer. If we are honest with the biblical description of the pastoral office we know that it is our duty to pray for the flock. But just as the world's best chef must also cook meals for himself, so too we must pray apart from our pastoral labors. There is no greater disconnect between knowledge and practice in the Christian life and ministry as there is between what the Bible says about prayer and how we actually pray.

One of the most terrifying indictments on prayerlessness is found in Jeremiah 17. This passage contains the often quoted words regarding the heart of man being deceitful and desperately wicked.

> Thus says the Lord: Cursed is the man who
>     trusts in man
> And makes flesh his strength,
> Whose heart departs from the Lord.

For he shall be like a shrub in the desert,
And shall not see when good comes,
But shall inhabit the parched places in the
    wilderness,
In a salt land which is not inhabited.
Blessed is the man who trusts in the Lord,
And whose hope is the Lord.
For he shall be like a tree planted by the
    waters,
Which spreads out its roots by the river,
And will not fear when heat comes;
But its leaf will be green,
And will not be anxious in the year of
    drought,
Nor will cease from yielding fruit.
The heart is deceitful above all things,
And desperately wicked;
Who can know it?
I, the Lord, search the heart, I test the
    mind,
Even to give every man according to his
    ways,
According to the fruit of his doings.

— JEREMIAH 17:5-10

The words of the prophet are painfully clear. God knows if we are dependent upon him or not. God sees us in private. He knows if we are looking to our wisdom, our training, our gifts, our personalities or if we are trusting in him. To trust in our own strength, our own flesh, is not merely a form of spiritual folly, it is a sign of our hearts departing from the Lord. The prophet emphasizes that our lives, and hence our ministries, will either bear the lush fruit of God's favor in answer to prayer or the shriveled evidence of self-trust.

What more could the God of heaven do to encourage us to pray than he has already done? He has shed the blood of his Son, given the gift of the Spirit of adoption, demonstrated the openness of his heart, and spoken of his generosity. He has spoken clearly of his desire to be known by his people and invited them into his presence at all times. How do we embrace the Bible's teaching about prayer, not just in regard to our calling, but in regard to our humanity? How do we attain and maintain a heart of communion and dependence? How do we keep it up over the decades? What, if anything, can be done to allow us to be like the man spoken of in Psalm 92 who bears fruit in old age and down through the years is still "fresh and flourishing?" Here are four things that come to mind to aid us in our private communion with the Lord and keep our souls warm for him.

## Staying Warm

The first thing that I would recommend is finding devotional aids that are calculated to deal with our hearts. There are books that not only bring light to your mind but heat to a cold heart. Men like Charles Spurgeon, Octavius Winslow, and JC Ryle were masters of conveying a warmth and passion for the Savior over decades of Christian service. These men retained their sense of wonder regarding the person and work of Christ, the love of God, the glories of redemption, and the joy of the world to come. They were not only excellent theologians, but they were pastors who obviously knew their own hearts and the hearts of the people to whom they ministered. Like any good pastor they knew both their Bible and the human condition.

A second encouragement if you find yourself growing dry and stale in your times with the Lord is to change things up a bit. If you've had the same Bible reading plan for twenty years, it may be time to experiment with a new way of Bible intake. After decades of seeking to go straight through the Bible in a year, I've taken some time to focus for a whole year on certain aspects of God's revelation. This past year my goal was to steep my mind in the New Testament by repetition. I've also incorporated listening to the Bible as a means of taking in God's word. Hearing the word from another voice, listening for the inflections and emphasis that man brings to his reading has often led me into unexpected times of reflection and meditation. You may want to break out a hymnal and either read or sing some great theology of the past. John Piper once said that, "It is in singing that our souls most closely approximate the joy and delight in divine truth that we are to seek after."[1]

Thirdly, we must honestly deal with this burden with the Lord. We must bring our cold or indifferent hearts to him. It may seem shameful that a preacher of the word should go to God and say, "I know you said that this book is worth more than much fine gold and its precepts are sweeter than honey and the honey comb, but Lord right now I'm not experiencing this joy—help me to come to this blessed book with freshness and eagerness."

The Bible claims to contain unsearchable riches. Every time we read it ought to bring us into contact with truths that we can never fully search out. No matter how well we know our Bibles, no matter how often we have read the word, we can ask the Lord to make the old things sweet as well as anticipate fresh discoveries.

Finally, there is no substitute for perseverance. Taking in God's word day by day is in many ways like the food that sustains our lives. We've all eaten a lot of forgettable meals. We may not have been keenly aware of the vitamins, minerals, and nutrients that coursed through our bodies as a result of downing that meal that was not particularly memorable or delectable in the moment. Sometimes the simple act of going to our Bibles again is what keeps us going. We may not push away from the table as full or as happy as we think we should, but it has brought us back to the Lord and spoken truth once more into our souls.

As is often noted, "The best of means are but means at best." Spending time in your Bible and prayer are a means of having your soul renewed. They are still the most powerful and reliable private means of grace to every follower of Jesus—pastors included. But ultimately, we are not kept by means. We will not praise means on the last day. Our hope and confidence in having our youth renewed like the eagle, in our running and not fainting, is in the Lord.

# PART IV

# PHYSICAL CARE FOR A PASTOR

BRIAN CROFT

# 10

## EAT

As a Southern Baptist Pastor, I try to attend the annual convention every year. It is important to be there, and I am able to see pastor friends I never see apart from this annual event. Besides, the Southern Baptist Convention always contains an unpredictability that is at times entertaining. For those unaware, this convention draws about 5,000-7,000 pastors and members of SBC churches all around the country. There is a portion of the convention that gives time for an open mic. In other words, anyone can get up on a mic and speak to a motion or issue. Anyone. As you might imagine, some interesting, sad, and contentious words have been said throughout the history of this denominational meeting.

One conversation on the open mic floor sticks out to me. It was a year where the older generation who had historically seen alcohol as a sin and destructive in every way was defending its position against a younger generation that didn't have the same convictions. In fact, the younger generation saw alcohol consumption as a gift from God if it was done responsibly and in moderation, citing no biblical command against alcohol, but against drunkenness. The conversation became intense and heated as one side spoke, then the other side responded. It felt like it was about to get out of hand, until a young thirty-year old pastor went to the mic and said:

> There is no one in this room that understands the devastating effects of alcohol like I do. I was raised by my dad. Single parent. He was an alcoholic. I had to take care of my dad as a child and watched him drink himself to death when I was fourteen years old. I wish I could forbid the use of alcohol, but the Bible doesn't allow me to do that. I do not want to shout where the Bible is silent.

Then, he bravely went where no Southern Baptist dares to go…

> This conversation saddens me. As I look around this room it appears an over-consumption of alcohol is not our major problem, but an enslavement and over consumption of food.

And with those piercing words, the elephant in the room of the largest protestant denomination in the world was escorted into center stage. There exists a massive obesity issue in the SBC, particularly with the pastors within the convention. In the eyes of some, being extremely overweight is endearing in a pastor as it is a sign they are loved and fed well, as in a similar way being fat in certain cultures is a sign of wealth. Nevertheless, it is a significant problem and doesn't just speak to the eating habits of pastors, but to the state of their soul. This chapter will consider the pastor's eating habits and how those habits can and do affect his own soul.

## Two Kinds of People

Here's a gross generalization to make a point. There are ultimately two kinds of people in this world and how they deal with stress:

Those who eat when they are stressed and those who don't eat when they are stressed. Food, and what we use it for, can be a very insightful gaze into the state of our souls. It is for me. I come from a long line of stress-eaters. Those who stress-eat cross the line of eating for enjoyment and providing nutrients for the body, to slide into that dangerous place of allowing food to be a means of comfort. I am convinced this is the main reason for the major obesity problem in America. As a result of the intense levels of stress pastors constantly endure, I am also convinced this is why so many pastors are overweight and unhealthy.

Let us also not miss the other side of this issue: those who avoid food to deal with stress. This soul exposure is more hidden because it doesn't parade as an obese, overworked pastor likely enslaved to food. Nevertheless, it causes a pastor to deal with the difficulties of the ministry in a way that is unhealthy for his physical body and ignoring the cry for help in his soul.

## Caring for the soul

How does a pastor come to realize not just his eating habits, but how food exposes the activity in his soul? Here are four ways to consider.

*First*, grow in awareness. Self-awareness is the most important tool for us to grow. Without knowing what the real problem is, we cannot address it. First, become aware of your family history and how you were taught to view and consume food. Was food a reward? Was food something used for comfort in difficult times in your home? Then each of us needs to be aware of how we use food now. It was a profound truth for me to realize food was a means of comfort for me in stress and anxiety. Until that realization came from God, I would just eat too much and not know why. It also brought a helpful insight to the other side of the spectrum when I was caring for women in my church who were struggling with eating disorders. The first step is coming to the realization that the way we view and consume food can reveal much about our souls.

*Second*, keep a close eye on your weight. I once heard Pastor Al Martin address a group of pastors and he shared this simple, but important, truth for pastors: "What you eat and what is not burned off that day goes here, here, and here [referring to parts of his body]." My weight has become a very helpful gauge on how well I am doing with my battle to find comfort in food. When my weight goes up it could mean a number of things. What it almost always exposes is that I am under more stress and eating more as a result. The managing of my weight becomes a gauge of not just stress level but how I am coping with it. If a pastor is fifty to one hundred pounds overweight, the cause may be a great turmoil in the soul that cannot be ignored.

However, weight does not tell the full story. I once talked with a pastor who battled overeating, and yet was very skinny. He lamented how hard it was to battle overeating, and yet hear often, "You are too skinny. You need to eat more." Likewise, there are those who are overweight because of a thyroid or metabolism issue, not because they overeat because of stress. Despite these exceptions, our weight can tell us a lot about our souls. Keep an eye on it.

*Third*, care about your personal testimony. Keeping one's weight down and staying in shape becomes harder the older we get. I'm not suggesting a person who has a bit of extra weight and doesn't exercise as often as they wished they did is in danger of marring their gospel testimony. Nor am I advocating that we are to somehow pursue an attractive exterior for our message to be heard. We are all broken vessels being used in the Master's hands. But, for any Christians to appear utterly enslaved to any kind of substance, whether it be drugs, possessions, or food, risks harming their testimony of freedom we have in the gospel. This was the elephant in the room at the convention that particular year that got exposed. The gospel provides freedom from sin and the world in Christ and the power of that message can become confusing when it is shouted by a man who is one hundred and fifty pounds overweight and gets winded walking to the pulpit to preach. Self-control is part of the fruit of the Spirit that needs to be born in our lives to affirm our testimony. The Apostle Peter calls all pastors to be examples to the flock (1 Peter 5:3). Be mindful of your personal testimony.

*Finally*, find your comfort in Jesus. It is a powerful thing to realize the impact food has on the soul and that we use food as a means of comfort in this fallen world. But, the solution doesn't stop by mere awareness. Our souls are nurtured and cared for when we realize our comfort in the stress and difficulties of our ministries is not in food, but in Jesus. We have to own our pursuit or rejection of food before Jesus can come and provide the only lasting comfort in the sufferings of this world. What resonates with the Holy Spirit who resides in each of us as followers of Jesus, is that Jesus satisfies in a way the best food cannot.

Pastors, be honest with the place food has in your life. It took me thirty years before I was honest about it. It will always be a battle for me. I assure you, the soul will continue to languish in the pain and sadness that exists that food tries to cover. Remember, God's grace will meet you in that place of openness and honesty and will give you strength to walk in self-control and victory with the snares that food brings. It will create a space in your soul that will bring the relief and peace that you truly seek.

# 11

## SLEEP

There is an incredible irony that exists in the lives of most busy people. The very thing we need to be highly productive and excel in the different aspects of our busy life is the first thing we sacrifice in the busyness—sleep. When you add a divine calling from God where God's people need care and God's kingdom is being built in the midst of the work of a pastor, sleep always seems less important. Before long, this mentality leads many pastors to see sleep as a hindrance to the work. The fact is, sleep is a gift from God. It reminds us we are not God, but humans who are frail, weak, and limited. When we neglect sleep, there is a physical price to pay, as David Murray writes:

> Just one week of sleeping fewer than six hours a night results in damaging changes to more than seven hundred genes, coronary narrowing, and signs of brain tissue loss. The latter is partly because sleep activates the brain's garbage disposal system, cleaning out toxins and waste products. Chronic sleep deprivation is associated with increased risk of infection, stroke,

cancer, high blood pressure, heart disease, and infertility. Sleep loss increases hunger, desire for larger portion sizes, and preference for high-calorie, high-carb foods, with the resulting risk of obesity. In short, sleeping is not a useless waste of time, but an essential biological need that prevents infection and helps us maintain healthy body weight.[1]

This cost doesn't stop at the physical, but infiltrates the mental, emotional, and the spiritual aspects of our lives. In other words, a lack of sleep harms our souls. This chapter aims to prove how essential it is that proper care for our souls as pastors involves getting a proper amount of sleep regularly each night. Let's first consider some reasons pastors in particular do not get the amount of sleep they need each night, then conclude with a few suggestions on how to pursue proper sleep as an effort to care for one's soul.

### Reasons pastors don't sleep

One reason pastors don't get the proper amount of sleep is because of pride. Pastors look at others around them who appear to be highly productive and do so on little sleep, and feel pressure to do the same. The reason I know this is because I felt it for many years. I fell into the trap so many do of hearing the stories of celebrated Christian leaders like Al Mohler or Joel Beeke reading twenty books a week on four to five hours of sleep a night. I knew I couldn't do that, but I didn't want to acknowledge that to anyone. I might look weak and incompetent. Pride makes us try to be someone we are not and God never intended us to be. The reality is I need eight hours of sleep a night. I won't just embrace that, but I will celebrate it now. I learned the world looks darker when we view it in a sleep-deprived state. Ministry is harder. My patience is thinner. I am not at my best on six hours and I know that. Pride causes pastors to do unwise things and not sleeping when we should is one of them.

Another reason pastors don't sleep is we deceive ourselves that doing something else is more spiritual. We could be studying, writing sermons, or praying throughout the night. Those sound so much more like spiritual tasks for a pastor, right? One of the most respected theologians in the world, Don Carson, has a different view:

> Sometimes the godliest thing you can do in the universe is get a good night's sleep—not pray all night, but sleep. I'm certainly not denying that there may be a place for praying all night; I'm merely insisting that in the normal course of things, spiritual discipline obligates you get the sleep your body needs.[2]

Sleep is a gift from God. It is not just one of the godliest things a pastor can do, but it is one of the wisest things we can do if we want to be at our best in our labors as a pastor each day.

The final reason pastors don't sleep is because we have no sense of control when we sleep. The control freak pastor has trouble sleeping and it isn't because he hasn't done enough spiritual tasks for the day, but he has trouble releasing control to the One who never sleeps or slumbers (Psalm 121:4). Pastors need to embrace that the gift of sleep each night is a call to faith that God is going to continue to be on the throne and rule while we sleep and will meet us with new mercies every morning when we awake.

## Caring for the soul

It is inaccurate to determine that sleep is simply a physical discipline that we submit to when we reach exhaustion. When pride, control, and confusion on what is truly godly behavior are in play, there is but one conclusion—this is a matter of the soul. How does a pastor care well for his soul in regard to the discipline of sleep?

We must first embrace our humanity. Just be honest about how much sleep you need. I need eight hours. You may need nine hours when another pastor only needs seven. Until you embrace that God has uniquely made you as a human being who is weak and needy for sleep, you will not be honest about how much you really need. One of the great differences between us and God is that we need sleep and he doesn't. There is freedom in embracing this truth and ministers to the weak and needy soul of a pastor in a special way.

Secondly, we must acknowledge the gift of sleep. Sleep should not be seen as something we just need to do when we are too exhausted to do anything else. Sleep is a gift from God as a way to recharge, to reset, so that we can be at our best to serve him tomorrow. Sleep is not a burden but a gift, and the pastor who acknowledges this will have a more peaceful soul.

Lastly, we must let go and trust Jesus. When we desire to control our lives, it is hard to let go of that. All sleep does for the Christian is remind us we are truly not in control. When we lie down to sleep we cannot escape that truth, even though we may have deceived ourselves all day about it. Pastors carry a tremendous amount of burden throughout the day. What a gift sleep can especially be for the pastor and his soul to relinquish those burdens to Jesus as we drift off to sleep.

I try to use my final moments before drifting off to sleep to say in my clear awareness of exhaustion this prayer to God:

God, I am reminded at this moment I am not God. I am only human. I need sleep. I can't do anymore right now. But you are God. You don't need sleep. You are all-powerful and everywhere. This moment is a gift as I get to sleep and let go of all these burdens I have carried for my people today. Help me to let go and give them over to you. Watch over me and my family tonight for you are a God that doesn't sleep or slumber. May your mercies be new tomorrow. Thank you.

Pastors, sleep is a gift. Embrace it. Use it each night to unburden your soul and bring you some temporary relief. I assure you, there will be plenty for your soul to bear in the morning.

## 12

# EXERCISE

I have been an athlete most of my life. I played every major sport until I got to high school. I played tennis in high school. I also played my first year in college. I wasn't much of a student, but sports I could do. And I loved them. Once I realized I wasn't going to be a professional tennis player, I started to spend my time focused on other things. I went on staff at a busy church one year after quitting college tennis while trying to finish my education. I knew exercise was still important, so I tried to continue being active. However, I was not as active as I was in previous years. Two things started to creep into my life.

First, I started to gain weight. This was a new experience for me as I was always fit from all the sports I had played. As my clothes started to feel mysteriously tight, I did what most people usually do in this moment—deny what was really happening. My clothes must be shrinking in the wash. I gained ten to fifteen pounds that next year and despite my best efforts to ignore it, others noticed. My father, who is a physician, came to me out of love and voiced his concern to me. It was in this moment where I first realized I was not being honest with myself about my clear weight gain. I was eating the same, but not as active as I once was.

Second, I started to feel stress in my life in a way I had not previously. I became aware of levels of anxiety I had never felt. I explained it away, knowing I was growing up and taking on adult-like responsibilities I had never had before. That was in play, but something else had changed. I was not exercising like before. The connection with weight gain was obvious, but could my lack of exercise affect how I deal with stress in my life?

As I reflect on this season of transition into adulthood in my early twenties, I realize the common link in my weight gain and added stress was the sudden absence of exercise in my life. It had always been there. It was like that childhood friendly companion that is so familiar to your life; you don't even realize how important he is until he is gone. That was exercise for me. It took years for me to realize what I now needed to do to care for myself in a new and fresh way if I was to survive ministry and adulthood. It is this same self-discovery that every pastor needs to realize if he is to care for his own soul well.

The problem is, when a pastor's schedule gets busy, it isn't food that gets cut out as a last priority. It isn't even sleep that gets squeezed out entirely. It's usually exercise. In all the priorities on a pastor's mind and heart, exercise seems to be the one we feel we can skip out on the most. This can only be explained in one way: We feel it is less necessary. And it is hard for many of us. This chapter seeks to give important reasons why exercise is still worth it and must be made a priority in a pastor's daily routine and how to accomplish this.

## Reasons pastors should exercise

The excuses we come up with to avoid exercise are endless. It hurts. I'm tired. I walked plenty today. I worked at my standing desk. I'll do it tomorrow. My body hurts. I pulled a hammy preaching Sunday. They are endless! And yet, when we neglect it, we miss a crucial way we care for ourselves not just physically, but emotionally and spiritually. Before I give a few reasons why exercise is so important, let me establish what I mean by exercise.

I am defining exercise by a mix of cardiovascular and strength training that must last at least twenty to thirty minutes. In other words, it must get your heart rate up to a certain point for a certain amount of time and must push your body physically in a way it doesn't get pushed the rest of the day. How that is achieved will vary according to individual tastes and abilities. For some the answer is membership of a local gym, for others cycling or a brisk walk up and down hills for thirty minutes in the neighborhood will be a good solution. There are good reasons to exercise. They all are connected to the care of one's soul.

The first reason is that exercise is a key element in weight management. We don't have to be fitness trainers to realize weight gain is the result of eating too much and not exercising enough. Finding the reason we over-eat and the reason we don't exercise is soul work. There is an element of self-discipline that comes with exercise, but the soul work is to consider why pastors allow themselves to continue in the pattern of overeating and never exercising. You need to consider that for you.

The second reason is that exercise is one of the best natural ways to relieve stress in our life. This is what I needed to discover in my early twenties. My body had become accustomed to having that natural release that a hard cardiovascular workout provided. All of a sudden, stress went up and that natural stress reliever disappeared. No wonder I was anxious. As I became aware of this benefit with exercise, I started to watch for it. Now, I can identify when my body feels tense from stress, know the signs, and usually a good hard run will remedy the tension. Even if you hate to exercise, try to measure your stress level before and after a workout to see the benefit for you.

The last reason is that exercise is simply good for you. God has created us in his image and has made our bodies in such a way that exercise helps that body. Pastor David Murray makes this exact point:

> Moderate physical exercise helps to expel unhelpful chemicals from our systems and stimulates the production of helpful chemicals. It strengthens not just the body but also the brain. Research has shown that walking just two miles a day reduces the risk of cognitive decline and dementia by 60 percent. And aside from the long-term benefits, exercise triggers the growth of new brain cells in the hippocampus and the release of neurotrophic growth factors—a kind of mental fertilizer that helps the brain grow, maintain new connections, and stay healthy. Exercise and proper rest patterns generate about a 20 percent energy increase in an average day, while exercising three to five times a week is about as effective as antidepressants for mild to moderate depression.[1]

Exercise is a good gift from God and is to be a help to our body, mind, heart, and soul. Pastors must make it a priority if we are to care for our souls well.

## Caring for our souls

You may have reached this point convinced that exercise hasn't been in its proper place in your life. You even see the effects of its absence and know you need to make a change. And yet, this can feel like a daunting task, especially for pastors who did not grow up as competitive athletes and cannot rely on that muscle memory to kick in at adulthood. Here are a few ways to help you get started.

First, do something small to start. Begin by going on a short walk in your neighborhood with your wife. The pattern of inactivity needs to be broken and it doesn't have to be through a goal to run a half-marathon next year. Just doing something begins to break the pattern. Set small achievable goals. Don't underestimate how something small in your regular daily routine will begin to bring the benefits God has designed us to gain from it.

Second, exercise with someone. This can be a great source of both motivation and accountability, especially for pastors trying to establish this in their life for the first time. It would be ideal for a pastor to find another pastor who would commit to meet three to four times a week at the gym or the park to exercise together. This will be a great reminder to both of you why this is important for the well-being of your souls. Don't miss the support and sounding board you can both be for each other in regard to ministry issues and struggles. I find it quite therapeutic and helpful to talk about ministry struggles while running, pounding out some pushups or hitting a heavy bag.

Finally, commit-long term. There's a reason the gyms and fitness centers of the world are packed the first week of January and return to normal six weeks later. Most people know exercise needs to be a part of their life, but fewer have the self-discipline and motivation to make it a part of their long-term lifestyle. It is crucial to a pastor's success that he implements a realistic exercise regimen into his busy life.

There's a ninety-five-year-old widow who walks a track near her home three days a week. Just five years ago she walked five miles each time. At ninety-five, she still walks four miles each time. She is amazing. When I asked her how she was able to keep this up, she said this:

I started a long time ago and I have just kept doing it. There are many days I don't feel like it, but I know as soon as I stop, my body will slow down. The key is doing something for your whole life and stick with it. It must be consistent, or it will never stick when you reach my age.

Pastors need to heed these words, not just for the sake of physical health, but so that we can be our strongest to serve Christ in our calling. We have been given one body and if we don't take care of it, it will hinder the noble work to which we have been called now, and certainly as we age. Regular exercise will be a help to our bodies and is essential to the well-being of our souls.

## 13

## FRIENDSHIP

Charles Spurgeon is one of my heroes. I love so many of the same things about Spurgeon that others commonly love about him, such as his Christ-centered preaching, his wit, humor, courage, authenticity, boldness, brilliance, and ministry faithfulness, to name a few. However, the more I learn about this prince of preachers, the more I feel drawn to some of the lesser-known qualities of this larger-than-life figure. As a very young man, he was one of the few pastors willing to go into the homes of those infected by the plague in London and care for the sick and dying. He was uniquely transparent about his struggles with depression. And another lesser-known mark of Spurgeon I have come to admire was his close, intimate friendships with other men—particularly pastors.

Iain Murray wrote a biography on Spurgeon's eventual successor, Archibald Brown. Brown pastored another large congregation on the other side of London from Spurgeon. There are a few moments in the book where Murray beautifully captures the sweet friendship that existed between Brown and Spurgeon. One aspect of Brown's suffering was the loss of two wives within a few years of the other. Brown later wrote about Spurgeon's care of him as he experienced the grief and despair of losing his second wife a few days previously:

> Broken with sore grief, I went over to the Metropolitan Tabernacle. I could not preach but I thought I could worship, and how amazed I was to find that he had prepared a sermon on purpose for me... As I turned round to come out at the close of the service, there was just one grip of his hand as he said, 'I have done all I can for you, my poor fellow.' I felt he had. I rode home with him that day, and had his loving fellowship as he sat with me during the afternoon.[1]

Years later when Spurgeon was just a few weeks from his own death, he penned this final letter to Brown:

> Beloved Brother, receive the assurance of my heart-love, although you need no such assurance from me. You have long been most dear to me; but in your standing shoulder to shoulder with me in protest against deadly error we have become more than ever one. The Lord sustain, comfort, perfect you! Debtors to free and sovereign grace, we will together sing to our redeeming Lord, world without end.[2]

News of Spurgeon's death reached Brown in London one day after he died. In Brown's sermon that next Sunday, he emotionally spoke about his dear friend who recently went to glory:

> He has been to me a very Elijah, and I have loved in any way possible to minister to him. Our roots have been intertwined for well nigh thirty years. Is it any wonder that I feel almost powerless this morning to think of him as a preacher, as an

orator, as an organizer, or as anything except the dearest friend I have ever known.[3]

Spurgeon and Brown were spiritual giants of their day, pastoring two of the largest churches in all of England. And yet, they both knew there was something they needed to survive the rigors of ministry and the personal suffering of their life— friendship. Not just any friendship, but a close, personal, intimate, and sacrificial pastor-to-pastor friendship that regularly turned each other's gaze to Jesus.

This chapter seeks to persuade every modern pastor of this essential need. It is a need that is not simply rooted in enjoyment and companionship, but in the necessity to care well for one's soul and survive a long-term ministry. As a pastor seeking meaningful friendship, I am commonly asked two questions:

Should a pastor find friends inside, or outside, his own church?

Should a pastor seek friendships primarily with pastors, or those not pastors?

Let's consider these two common questions and then move to ponder how pastors can begin to seek the kinds of deep, meaningful friendships that are good for their souls.

## Finding meaningful friendships

Pastors should seek friendships both inside and outside the church. The church can be a lonely place if the pastor doesn't have friends of some kind within it. It is sweet to have fellow pastors and other leaders with whom the pastor serves to enjoy the fellowship of one another.

Comradery in the rigors of local church ministry is invaluable. And yet, the role of the pastor in a church can make it difficult to find relationships where he can be completely open, honest, and transparent in certain areas. It can be difficult to share all thoughts and opinions with people in your own church. Therefore, friendships outside a pastor's own local church are very helpful, even necessary. These provide a place of safety to talk about issues. It brings relational relief from the burden of always relating to others as the pastor. It produces an environment where church life is not the first conversation. It requires effort, but pastors are most helped by having friends inside, as well as outside his own local church.

Pastors should seek friendships with both other pastors and those who are not pastors. One of the most significant gifts from God to me as a pastor are other pastors. The ministry is a uniquely hard work and only a pastor knows what it is like to be a pastor. As a result, there exists a special fraternity of men who serve as pastors, which naturally creates bonds of friendship that can be deep and meaningful—like Brown and Spurgeon.

On the other hand, I have found a great deal of joy with friends who are not pastors, especially outside my church. One of my dearest friends is a Chick-fil-A owner and a layman in a very different church from mine. We enjoy a lot of the same things, but what I appreciate most about him is he is my friend because he loves me, not because I'm his pastor or for what I can give to him or do for him. Ultimately, this is what all pastors desire in friendship, someone to love them for who they are as a person, not for what they can do for them. Most of the pastor's relationships revolve around the care they extend to others. That is the call of a pastor. However, it can make finding open, honest, transparent, meaningful, mutually beneficial friendships hard to find.

## Pursuing friendships good for the soul

The most important way for a pastor to find a meaningful friendship is to pursue being the kind of friend he seeks. Here are three qualities that can make any friendship more meaningful, but

I would argue they are particularly important for the unique relationship pastors have with others.

First, pastors need to be an example of a good, faithful friend. Too often it is hard for a pastor to know who wants him for who he is, or for what he can give them. I can relate to this dilemma as most people in my life love and appreciate me for what I can give them. This makes for very fulfilling ministry, but a challenge to find mutual and meaningful friendships. A pastor needs to take a risk and be that faithful friend to someone else with the hope it will be returned. Be there for others in friendship and it is in that space a pastor might find a true friend.

Second, pastors need safety in friendship. Pastors need a place to go where they are received just as their loving Savior receives them. That is, received in love, compassion, empathy, understanding, wisdom and truth. Pastors need a place where they can be open and honest in their struggles, sins, fears, temptations. We need a place where someone refrains from judging and fixing, and simply listens. We need a place to be sad, angry, hurt, and broken. We need another man to walk through the valleys and anguish of our complicated, pressure-filled lives. We need someone who will love us deeply, and yet point us to the One who loves us more than we can imagine and laid down his life for us. Look for those kinds of relationships, and the best way to find them is to be that open, compassionate, listener to another. One of the greatest gifts God has given me to minister to my soul is another safe pastor who desires this kind of mutual friendship.

Last, pastors need an unwavering commitment in friendship. We have all been hurt by someone who couldn't take the brokenness and baggage we brought into a friendship and it ends. We are left hurt, cynical, and guarded for the next time. This can be most dangerous for pastors as these kinds of open friendships already require an extra effort and carry with them a level of liability unique from others. Pastors are often rejected and criticized by church members who leave the church mad at something the pastor has done. This fear of rejection can easily be carried over into friendships even outside the church. Be a committed friend who will not be scared away by sins, brokenness, and the realities of our humanity. As you are that kind of friend where you embrace the brokenness of someone else and love them no matter what, it will probably be in that place of commitment you will find the same commitment of another.

In an amazing irony, the one who arguably needs a friend the most for the good of his soul finds it most difficult to find one—a pastor. Pastors also need those to care for their soul. It will take effort. It will require risk. Pastors will be tempted at times to think it is not worth it. Many pastors spend a lifetime in ministry with very few genuine friends. And yet, I want to urge you to seek them, not just for the unique enjoyment of pastoral friendships and companionship in a noble but lonely calling, but for the good it is to the soul.

## 14

# SILENCE

I've spent most of my adult life hating silence—and didn't know it. It was a major blind spot. I always dismissed my desire to be with people and avoid being alone as part of being an extrovert and loving people. I excused my talkative nature to my heightened relational instincts. These qualities also seemed to help my interactions with people as a pastor, so I thought nothing more of it. It wasn't until I began my own counseling journey out of a personal crisis where I was confronted with this long-held deception in my life.

My counselor observed some behavior in my life that went unnoticed by most, but became flags of concern for him. He saw that I ran from being alone. He realized I was uncomfortable in silence and didn't know what to do with it. He experienced the way I often dominated conversations with my words. This also exposed my terrible listening skills, which he was wise and winsome enough to connect to my silence issues. So, he began to press me in this area and it was difficult. In fact, it led to an implosion of my soul and began the process of healing it desperately needed.

It was through this journey that I learned if my emotions are the gateway to my soul, then it is silence that exposes the soul. I was not ready to face the ugly things that got exposed. But God in his amazing grace met me in a sweet, powerful way and began a healing journey that has brought a consistent peace in my soul. It was through silence in a quiet place, meditating on truth, and prayerfully asking the Lord's help that I experienced this deeper level of God's grace and presence within my soul. It is the same place that every pastor must expose and reach with the power of God's grace for us to experience his love deeply and, as a result, have a long ministry.

This silence I am advocating for in the pastor's life is not some form of secular meditation, but a biblical silence and solitude. Don Whitney considers it a significant spiritual discipline of the Christian life.[1] It is a stillness that allows us to grow more aware of our soul's activity as the Holy Spirit lives and works in us. It is a discipline by which we commune with Jesus, become more powerfully aware of his truth and presence, and more receptive to his unending grace. Puritan scholar Joel Beeke articulates well the kind of meditation that fosters this experience:

> Puritan meditation engages the mind with God's revealed truth in order to inflame the heart with affections towards God and transform the life unto obedience. Thomas Hooker defined it like this: 'Meditation is a serious intention of the mind whereby we come to search out the truth, and settle it effectually upon the heart.' The direction of our minds reveals the truest love of our hearts, and so, Hooker said, he who loves God's Word meditates on it regularly (Psalm 119:97). Therefore, Puritan meditation is not repeating a sound, emptying the mind, or imagining physical sights and sensations, but a focused exercise of thought and faith upon the Word of God.[2]

God commands that we be still and know he is God (Psalm

46:10). The Psalmist reminds us our souls are to go into silence and wait on God alone (Psalm 62:1-5). Jesus regularly went off to a solitary place to pray and be still (Mark 1:35; Luke 5:16; Matthew 14:13). Silence and solitude is a biblical discipline of the Christian life every Christian needs. Pastors are no different.

This chapter seeks to not only call every pastor to the discipline of regular silence and solitude in his life, but to see this is an essential piece to the care of a pastor's soul. First, let's consider the reasons for silence in our life, then turn to the practical of how to begin to embrace it amidst a busy and noisy ministry.

## Reasons for Silence

Most of us can agree on some obvious reasons for silence, such as we all need quiet, time to get refocused, time alone with God, time to pray and read God's word, and less distractions. However, I would like to give four reasons that are less obvious and connect more so to silence being a catalyst to care for one's soul.

First, silence exposes the soul. A common defense mechanism is to use busyness and noise to avoid pain in our lives. It could be unresolved pain and abuse from the past, or it could be a current suffering. Regardless, noise and distraction can give the illusion it isn't there, or that it has no power. Silence can expose that deep pain and demonstrate its undeniable presence in our souls. It is when we are still and silent that we become more aware of our emotions, what our minds obsess over, and the physical pain we feel that could be related to stress and anxiety.

Second, silence confronts the voices. The voices to which I refer are the messages we hear about ourselves. We all have them. They are voices from those throughout our life. They are the messages the enemy loves to whisper in our ears. They are the interpretive messages of those presently in our life. When those voices are harsh, abusive, and lie about our value and identity in Christ, they become very unpleasant to hear and we do what we must to run from them. These voices tormented me. Abusive voices from my past, lies from the enemy, and painful words of criticism in the present all created these messages of failure and self-loathing that were loudest when I was alone in silence. So, I ran from silence to try and escape these voices. I needed silence to confront these voices and speak powerful, gospel truth against the lies I heard and had believed for so long. Martyn Lloyd Jones has famously addressed these voices in the context of depression, stating:

> The main trouble in this whole matter of spiritual depression in a sense is this, that we allow our self to talk to us instead of talking to our self. Am I just trying to be deliberately paradoxical? Far from it. This is the very essence of wisdom in this matter. Have you realized that most of your unhappiness in life is due to the fact that you are listening to yourself instead of talking to yourself?[3]

Silence allows us to confront the reality that when we listen to ourselves instead of talking to ourselves we consequently say harsh, soul-crushing words.

Third, silence teaches us to listen. It was a troubling discovery when I realized how long I had been a pastor yet was still a poor listener. I listened, but it was to prepare to respond. I needed to learn to listen without a need to respond. Just listen and empathize. As I began to embrace silence, I realized I was learning to listen also. I heard sounds around me I never noticed before. I felt more receptive to the message of God's word. It is amazing what happens when you are not so preoccupied with trying to figure out what to say or do next. Just listen.

Finally, silence tests our need for noise. I thought I just loved people and activity. I had no idea that I needed noise because my soul was tormented in silence. Silence exposes the soul and can test how much we have grown to depend on noise to block out the pain of our lives. This is one of the many reasons why we all need blocks of time away from our phone, email, social media, and every electronic device that creates much of the constant source of noise in our life. Pastors do not have to make much effort to find noise and distraction in their life. But silence is another matter. We must fight for it. Silence challenges us to face that pain and allow the power of the gospel to penetrate deep in our souls and begin to find healing. And yet, how does a pastor begin to embrace silence out of care for his soul?

## Embracing Silence

While away on a silent retreat, I was reminded of these words found in a room dedicated to silence and solitude:

> The role of silence was deemed to be important here, as a means of ensuring that one did not fritter away precious but demanding leisure through acedia and small talk. Communities which respect human growth probably need to make explicit provision for solitude, otherwise a potential source of enrichment is lost.

Although I hated silence, I slowly came to realize I needed to make "explicit provision for solitude" for the sake of my soul. As a result, I was led through a three-step process that helped me come to not just realize I needed silence, but caused me to eventually long for it. That three-step process is daily practice, extended times of silence, and scheduled retreats.

First, a pastor must begin by establishing a short daily silence. The Psalmist writes for us to be still and know God is God (Psalm 46:10). Small, but regular goals are the key. Don't underestimate the value of carving out five to ten minutes a day where you sit in silence with no music playing, no phone ringing, and no people talking. Just sit and take in the quiet. Be aware of God's presence. Know he is God. Pray. Listen to what is around you. I seek this daily experience often on my back porch outside where I go and close my eyes, feel the breeze, hear the leaves rustle, listen to the birds and animals move. Most of all, receive God's grace as you ponder his favor and love towards you. Recite gospel truth to yourself (Ephesians 2:1-10; Romans 5:6-11). Center yourself with just you and Jesus before others bombard the remainder of the day. Even if it is just five minutes of silence a day, I find this time invaluable when the rest of my day if full of people and noise. Five minutes each day is better than thirty minutes only once.

Next, a pastor needs to find more extended times of silence. The Psalmist reminds us our souls are to go into silence and *wait* on God alone (Psalm 62:1-5). We cannot rush waiting. It takes more time. This could be one hour a week where you are away from all noise and people to be alone with God. As the short, daily silence helps keep you centered for the day, this more extended time is what I find more restful and restorative for my soul. This typically happens in my life on Monday mornings when I go on a run on a hiking trail away from people. After my run, I just sit in the quiet with God, aware of his glory in Creation all around me in the woods or near a pond. I remain still and know he is God and I am not (Psalm 46:10). And I wait for God alone (Psalm 62:1-5). For others, it might be finding a quiet room in the house after the kids go to school. Whatever works for you, be intentional about scheduling this time in your week. You will not stumble on it. Jesus modeled intentionality to go away alone in solitude and pray (Mark 1:35). If the daily silence keeps us going for the day, this extended time at least once a week is what God often uses to restore our souls to him and reminds us of his grace at work in us.

Finally, a pastor should move to scheduling one to two silent retreats each year. It is here where you will discover how you truly feel about silence. I did. This could be an overnight trip somewhere, but doesn't have to be. I have scheduled my silent retreats to be during the day where I will leave early in the morning and return for dinner with my family. This pursuit of silence takes the care of your soul to another level, for it exposes how much you need noise, people, busyness, and distraction. An all-day silent retreat will expose much, including what you use noise to run from in your life. My silent retreats have become a gut-check of things hidden in my soul from which I try to run by busyness in my life. Every pastor needs something that will press those hidden things, causing him to be confronted with them before God, and time to stop and receive his grace and forgiveness.

Jesus has set us free from the power of sin, shame, and death, and has rescued us from the wrath of God we deserve. It is all by grace through faith. Our identity is now in Christ and we are eternally adopted children of the one true God. We have the Holy Spirit of God indwelling each of us by faith, making us more like Jesus every day. And yet, so many Christians fail to experience deeply in their souls the power of God's grace in the gospel. This includes pastors. This was me most of my ministry and it took an awareness of my own soul and how to gain access to it so that powerful grace in the gospel would permeate in those deep, dark places. Silence with biblical meditation is a wonderful tool and gift from God to bring that awareness. We can only shepherd our people to the places to which we have personally gone and experienced. Embrace silence with meditation as that peaceful, healing balm for your noisy, restless soul.

# 15

# REST

One of the greatest hindrances to the passionate, driven, highly productive modern pastor is an inability to know how to rest. I can relate. For most of my adult life, I didn't know how to rest. In fact, what I now understand as rest and recreation I saw as laziness and lack of productivity. After all the kingdom of God is being built! Who has time to rest? I learned every pastor needs to rest. I did. Otherwise our souls are not given a space to breathe and re-group from the grind of ministry. I came to understand rest as essential and that it comes in the form of three layers as a formula for a long and fruitful ministry. Those three layers are a day off, vacation, and sabbatical.

## A Day Off

Some like to question whether a pastor should take a day off. Let me be clear for those who are curious—yes! Every pastor should take a day off every week. Additionally, it ideally needs to be a day other than Saturday. Here are a few reasons.

Sunday is a work day for a pastor. I know it is the Lord's

Day. I know some pastors are preaching on Sunday and some are not. Regardless, while most are getting a break from their weekly grind on Sunday, the pastor is experiencing the pinnacle of it. Sunday is a joyful day, but it is also an emotionally draining day and is far from being low-key and restful.

A pastor never really leaves work. Regardless how we spend our evenings or how hard we try, the pastor never completely checks out. Even if the phone does not ring or no one stops by, the sermon is still on the mind and heart, that elderly saint's battle with cancer still weighs on the shoulders, and there just is not a clock we ever punch that magically causes us to forget about the burdens of caring for souls until 9:00 am the next morning. Although the burdens never completely leave, a day where we can try to focus on our families and escape the daily grind is invaluable for our souls and long term ministry stamina.

A pastor needs a weekly day where his family comes first and they know it. There are many sacrifices and crosses to bear for the pastor's family. Because of this, taking a day when they know they will be "dad's focus" helps them give dad up to the busyness of the other days. There are fewer effective ways to communicate your love for your family than for them to know there is a day for them, it is scheduled regularly, and regardless of the craziness, it is coming soon.

One of the best decisions I have ever made for the benefit of my family and ministry has been to commit to a day off every week. Only funerals and true emergencies cause me to compromise it. My day off is Friday because it fits best in our schedule. Pick a day that works best for you and your family. The point is pick a day. Let your family and church know when that will be and stick to it. I still manage to work about fifty to sixty hours a week with a day off. My family looks forward to it. Your family will too if you schedule it in your week and honor it. Little decisions like committing to a day off every week are crucial to the long-term care of your soul.

## Vacation

Some might believe I will suggest how many weeks of vacation you should be given by your church, or how much you should advocate for your vacation time. My concern is not about how much vacation time a pastor is given, but how he uses (or doesn't use) what he is given.

This is an appropriate time to pause for a confession. I often fail at my own advice. Just thought I would acknowledge that in case you think I write this way because I have figured it all out. Far from it. The stewardship of my vacation time has been a glaring area of failure in my life that I have tried to address the last several years.

A couple of years ago, I was lovingly confronted by a dear friend and fellow pastor that I was not using all my vacation time. In his rebuke, he explained to me the reasons I should be taking every day of vacation the church gives me, which I had never done. Here was the basis for his thoughtful, insightful, and wise argument:

It's for you. The pastor never gets a break in the regular routine. We are constantly on call. Vacation time is that time where you get time to breathe away from the madness, be refreshed, and rest. All of us who are pastors know we are no good for our people when we are exhausted, distracted, and mentally and emotionally spent. Use the time and use it wisely to achieve that end.

It's for your family. Your family always has to share you. During vacation, your family has a blocked amount of time where they don't have to share you with the church. When you don't use all your time that has already been approved by the church for this purpose, you rob your family of having your sole focus to care for, fellowship with, and enjoy them.

It's for your church. How is it that many of our churches have somehow existed and functioned for the last fifty to one hundred years without us? Yet all of a sudden, we come and develop this complex that our church can now no longer live without us for a week or two. Using all your vacation time forces others to step up in your absence, shows them they can make it without you for a time, and reminds the pastor most of all that God is not utterly dependent on him for this church to function. We are expendable, and we need regular jolts of humility to remind us of that.

## Sabbatical

A practice common among some like-minded churches is to grant full-time pastoral staff occasional pastoral sabbaticals. During a sabbatical, a pastor sets aside regular pastoral duties (i.e., preaching, teaching, worship, member care, and administration) to focus his time and energy on other profitable tasks. I was given a sabbatical at the completion of ten years as Senior Pastor of my church. No pastor had ever taken a sabbatical in the eighty-year history of our church. As a result, my fellow pastors felt a need to explain to the congregation what this foreign idea was. Here's the description of what they presented to our congregation:

The intention of a pastoral sabbatical is to provide a time of rest, renewal, and refreshment of the pastor's soul and his family with longevity of ministry in mind. The pastoral sabbatical includes deliberate efforts for the pastor to grow, learn, mature, and excel all the more in his ministry upon his return. The pastoral sabbatical is distinct from vacation time. When the pastor uses vacation time, he is not expected to fulfill ministry obligations. However, during the pastoral sabbatical, the pastor is charged to engage in devotional, theological, pastoral, and personal reflection and renewal.

A sabbatical can take on various forms and lengths. To see the full explanation of my two-month sabbatical and how it was presented to our congregation, see Appendix A. What is important to realize for this context is seeing another layer of rest that is essential for proper care of a pastor's soul and a healthy formula for a long ministry.

The fight for rest in these three layers is real. The pastor must fight to see his own need for this kind of rest and reject the lie that if he's not doing ministry he's being a bad steward of his calling. Additionally, there is the pressure of the congregation that comes into play. Is the pastor being lazy? Why does he need three months off when I only get two weeks? Because of these pressures, a common result is the pastor doesn't rest. He just keeps going. And going. And going. Until he breaks and has no idea how he got there. Pastors, fight for your rest. And when you rest, let go. Submit it all to the Chief Shepherd. Allow him to revive your tired and anxious soul.

# CONCLUSION

Our hope is that this book has brought a greater sense of awareness for you of the activity of your own soul; an awareness of your calling from God; an awareness of the pressures you face and how they might affect you; an awareness of your own need for care, not simply your flock. Ultimately, our desire for you is captured in the words of the Apostle Paul to the Corinthians:

> But I call God as witness to my soul, that to spare you I did not come again to Corinth. Not that we lord it over your faith, but are workers with you for your joy; for in your faith you are standing firm.
>
> — 2 CORINTHIANS 1:23-24

Our heart's desire for you before God is comparable to Paul's desire for the Corinthians:

> We are workers with you.
> We labor for your joy.

So you might stand firm.

The writing of this book was helpful for us both as we considered how we have been helped by these biblical and practical ideas put forward. We reflected on our own personal joys and struggles and how gracious God has been to us both to allow us a long ministry with the hope of many years to come. But our chief aim was for this book to remind you we are workers with you in this difficult but noble task. We seek to stand firm with you, and finish the race well, not merely to crawl across the finish line. We desire for you the special and unique joy that comes from being an undershepherd of our great Chief Shepherd, Jesus Christ.

Pastors, press on in this challenging, but privileged task we have been given to care for souls. Spend and be spent in the service of our bountiful Master. End each day knowing your labors are not in vain and that they have a great, eternal purpose. But do not neglect the care of your own soul. Take heed to yourself. Remember all the gifts of God and means of grace he has given us to nurture our own souls so that we are sharp and attentive to care for others.

Our calling is to care for souls, the souls of others as well as our own. Let us do this with great diligence so that we finish our race well, not just with a satisfaction in our ministry labors, but a peaceful soul that knows for certain we have indeed known and walked with Jesus every step of the way.

# APPENDIX A: SABBATICAL EXAMPLE

Pastoral sabbatical recommendation to the church (example):

## Motion

We, the pastors, move to grant Senior Pastor Brian Croft a pastoral sabbatical from June 1, 2013, through July 31, 2013.

## Definition

A practice common among some like-minded churches is to grant full-time pastoral staff occasional pastoral sabbaticals. During a sabbatical, a pastor sets aside regular pastoral duties (i.e., preaching, teaching, worship, member care, and administration) to focus his time and energy on other profitable tasks.

## Description

The intention of a pastoral sabbatical is to provide a time of rest, renewal, and refreshment of the pastor's soul and his family with longevity of ministry in mind. The pastoral sabbatical includes deliberate efforts by the pastor to grow, learn, mature, and excel all the more in his ministry upon his return. The pastoral sabbatical is distinct from vacation time. When the pastor uses vacation time, he is not expected to fulfill ministry obligations. However, during the pastoral sabbatical, the pastor is charged to engage in devotional, theological, pastoral, and personal reflection and renewal.

Upon approval of the sabbatical from the congregation, Pastor Brian will develop a deliberate plan and clear agenda for the sabbatical time. This plan will include:

Praying for and seeking wisdom and direction for coming years of faithful ministry at Auburndale;

Reading several books from topics of interest and need that will challenge him as a pastor, preacher, and writer;

Focusing on the preaching of an admired, model pastor and noting insights from that pastor's preaching style and techniques;

Meeting with a few older pastors to receive instruction on ministerial faithfulness and fruitfulness;

Attending other churches to hear other preachers and learn about ministry initiatives; and

Limiting external preaching, speaking, and teaching engagements to protect the time given for pastoral renewal. The recommendation of the other pastors is a limit of two such engagements.

## Rationale

The other pastors recommend the pastoral sabbatical for a number of reasons. First, the timing of the sabbatical will occur close to Pastor Brian's tenth anniversary (September 2013). We have made the motion, in part, to give the congregation an opportunity to express gratitude and exude generosity toward our pastor. Second, the pastoral sabbatical will benefit the congregation. Our expectation is that Pastor Brian's focus on devotional, theological, pastoral, and personal reflection and renewal will bear fruit at Auburndale. Third, the pastors feel a need for a ministerial and theological vision for the work of our church in the Auburndale community. Ministry has changed in the ten years since Brian arrived. Not only is ministry different after ten years, but, by God's grace, through Brian, it is more expansive and fruitful.

## Logistics

Pastor Brian will be released from the regular pastoral duties of preaching, teaching, worship leadership, member care, and administration during the two-month pastoral sabbatical. The other pastors of Auburndale will collaborate to ensure that these duties are appropriately delegated and diligently fulfilled. In the event of an emergency, the pastors reserve the right to modify the terms of this proposal to ensure the faithful care of members of Auburndale.

# APPENDIX B: 10 STEPS TO A MORE FRUITFUL SABBATICAL

**Written two months after my return from a two-month sabbatical:**

I recently returned from sabbatical. My church totally relieved me of duty for the months of June and July. I was banned from Sunday services at our church and was kept in the dark about pastoral issues they faced during this two-month period.

Leading up to this time, I sought counsel from many pastors who had been given similar time off. I was struck by how many shared of different regrets once their time was done. So I tried to use my sabbatical in the most fruitful way possible. Here are a few lessons I learned.

1) Delight in your wife. Have plenty of date nights. Care for her. Study her. Learn from her. Laugh with her. Enjoy her. Reflect on your years of ministry together. Realize she needs this time as much as you do. Resolve to make it a great benefit to her soul. Seize time

to delight in her while the busyness that often cuts into your time together is temporarily relieved.

2) Enjoy your kids. I have never before had such an extended period where I could focus on time with my kids. I needed to make sure they were not only a primary focus, but that my heart was taking in this time with them and truly enjoying them. Many pastors expressed regret to me on this front. So we spent time at the pool, parks, out of town a bit, reading, wrestling, laughing, riding bikes, and whatever else they wanted to do.

3) Be intentional with spiritual disciplines. I committed to have times of reading God's Word that were long and covered large portions of text. I usually spend most of my time "staring at the trees" for sermon preparation; for this break I allowed "the forest" to feed my soul.

I also had intentional times of silence and prayer for the sake of my own soul, asking God for guidance on a vision for our church for the next ten years, as I've just finished up my first ten as pastor. Additionally, I renewed a helpful discipline I've neglected: journaling. Embrace the basic spiritual disciplines we exhort our people to engage in that we can often let slide in our own lives.

4) Be consistent with physical disciplines. Commit to sleeping eight hours a night. Try to renew regular exercise—for me, this meant a three to four day a week workout plan. And resolve to eat well. If you do none of these well in your normal grind, a sabbatical can be a great time to recommit to stewarding your body and energy well. I lost ten pounds on my sabbatical and was reminded how much sleep I actually need to be at my best to serve

the Lord. Do not underestimate how poorly you care for your body during the grind of ministry.

5) Be mentored by a faithful dead pastor. Dead pastors from different moments in history can teach us about pastoral ministry in ways modern pastors cannot. I chose the great eighteenth century English Particular Baptist Andrew Fuller (1754-1815) to mentor me during this time via his writings. It was so encouraging! Pick one, then immerse yourself in his life and ministry and allow him to teach you.

6) Learn about preaching from a faithful living pastor. I chose Ted Donnelly, who pastored in Northern Ireland for over 35 years until his health recently declined. He is known in Britain as one of the most gifted, Spirit-filled preachers in the last half century. I listened to his sermons and learned much. God also fed my soul through his Word in the process. Choose someone you don't know very well but who would be a helpful instructor to push you to grow in your preaching.

7) Visit other churches. It can certainly be restful and encouraging to worship among your people with your regular pastoral duties relieved. But the inevitable conversations that will arise can make a sabbatical less of a break if you spend Sundays in your own church. So I made sure my responsibilities at church were covered so that I could worship at other churches for the entire sabbatical.

If you go to other solid churches where the Word is preached you will experience Christian fellowship. There is much to learn from other churches and pastors. You may experience something in their public gathering you then choose to bring back to your church. If you do not have many choices, pick a couple of solid churches during your sabbatical where you can simply attend, relax, and be fed while sitting with your family.

8) Put off the tasks you normally put on. A sabbatical will not be truly restful if you hang on to what normally wears you down. This is why my fellow pastors banned me from writing a book or preaching anywhere, both of which are a normal part of my ministry. Although many take sabbatical time to write—which is fine for some—my fellow pastors were right to forbid me from doing so. Make sure you are honest with yourself about the things that wear on you. And make sure to set them down for this time, even if they are things you love to do.

9) Play golf. Golf is relaxing yet humbling for most of us. There are layers of reasons this is good for your soul. I shot some of my best rounds of golf in years during my sabbatical and beat my very competitive father for the first time in my life. Clearly, the favor of the Lord was upon me. If not golf, find some other relaxing, humbling way to have fun that's tough to fit into your regular grind.

10) Truly rest. I typically don't rest well. But I realized through others' counsel that if I came to the end of my time off and my wife and I did not feel refreshed and rested, we would have defeated the purpose of this gift from our church and squandered this opportunity. Whatever will help you rest from the rat race of your regular labors and refresh your soul is what you should do.

If you are planning for an upcoming sabbatical, I hope this begins a helpful conversation between you and your fellow pastors about what would be the best way for you to benefit from this gift. Be intentional. Involve others in your church to help determine the best way for you to spend your time. Listen to your wife's input. And pray God would grant you to rest well and wisely, so that fond memories vastly outweigh regrets when you return to the normal routine of ministry.

# NOTES

## 1. Take Heed To Yourself

1. C.H. Spurgeon, *Lectures to My Students* (Grand Rapids, MI: Zondervan Publishing House, 1954), 2.
2. C.H. Spurgeon, *Lectures to My Students* (Grand Rapids, MI: Zondervan Publishing House, 1954), 11.

## 5. Awakening

1. Richard Baxter, *The Reformed Pastor*, ed. William Brown (Edinburgh: Banner of Truth, 2001), 53.
2. Charles Bridges, *The Christian Ministry: An Inquiry into the Causes of its Inefficiency* (Edinburgh: Banner of Truth, 1967), p. 91-92.
3. C.H. Spurgeon, *Lectures to my Students* (Grand Rapids, MI: Zondervan Publishing House, 1954), 26.
4. Spurgeon, *Lectures to my Students*, 26-27.
5. Thomas K. Ascol ed., *Dear Timothy: Letters on Pastoral Ministry*. (Cape Coral, FL: Founders Press, 2004), 272.

## 7. Love

1. Quote taken from http://www.unimedliving.com/men/relationship/real-men-don-t-cry.html

## 9. Embracing the Private Means of Grace

1. John Piper, Desiring God Blog, December 28, 1997.

## 11. Sleep

1. David Murray, *Reset: Living a Grace-paced Life in a Burnout Culture* (Wheaton, IL: Crossway, 2017), 56.

2. Don Carson, *Scandalous: The Cross and Resurrection of Jesus* (Wheaton, IL: Crossway, 2010), 147.

## 12. Exercise

1. David Murray, *Reset: Living a Grace-paced Life in a Burnout Culture* (Wheaton, IL: Crossway, 2017), 78-79.

## 13. Friendship

1. Iain H. Murray, *Archibald G. Brown: Spurgeon's Successor* (Edinburgh: Banner of Truth, 2011), 98.
2. Ibid, 144.
3. Ibid, 145.

## 14. Silence

1. See Don Whitney's classic book, *Spiritual Disciplines of the Christian Life*.
2. https://www.challies.com/reading-classics-together/the-practice-of-meditation/.
3. Martyn Lloyd Jones in *Spiritual Depression*.